Through the Eyes of the Heart

Through the Eyes of the Heart

Stories of Love and Loss

DAN FESTA

RESOURCE *Publications* • Eugene, Oregon

THROUGH THE EYES OF THE HEART
Stories of Love and Loss

Copyright © 2016 Dan Festa. All rights reserved. Except for brief quotations in critical publications or reviews, no part of this book may be reproduced in any manner without prior written permission from the publisher. Write: Permissions, Wipf and Stock Publishers, 199 W. 8th Ave., Suite 3, Eugene, OR 97401.

Resource Publications
An Imprint of Wipf and Stock Publishers
199 W. 8th Ave., Suite 3
Eugene, OR 97401

www.wipfandstock.com

PAPERBACK ISBN 13: 978-1-4982-3832-8
HARDCOVER ISBN 13: 978-1-4982-3834-2

Manufactured in the U.S.A. 02/23/2016

Contents

Acknowledgements | vii
Introduction | ix

Chapter 1
Too Young | 1

Chapter 2
A Fish Named Rudolph | 4

Chapter 3
Leather Restraints | 7

Chapter 4
A Book of Poems | 10

Chapter 5
A Babysitter | 13

Chapter 6
Pizza Delivery | 17

Chapter 7
One of Our Own | 20

Chapter 8
Alone | 24

Chapter 9
Blind | 30

Chapter 10
Black Ice | 35

Chapter 11
A Granddame | 39

Chapter 12
A Live Oak Tree | 43

Chapter 13
A New Roof | 53

Chapter 14
After Hours | 57

Chapter 15
Business as Usual | 62

Chapter 16
Engaged | 71

Chapter 17
I-95 Southbound | 77

Chapter 18
One Train Track Too Many | 82

Chapter 19
The Smell of Flesh | 88

Chapter 20
Jailed | 93

Epilogue | 99

Acknowledgements

I owe a huge debt of gratitude to the thousands of individuals who have shaped my life and helped me to become all that I am. I especially would like to thank all of the patients and families with whom I have had the honor of working. It truly was a privilege. I would like to thank the staff of the Medical University of South Carolina where I received my first "real" job; Pat W., Agnes A., Caroline S., Pat C., Gloria R., Vicky M., Stevie K., and Kathy V.

I would like to thank my mother who shaped in me the love of learning and encouraged me to think bigger thoughts and ideas. The early nurture and embracing love of my grandparents Violet and Paul D.; Margaret and John M., who broadened my world and gave me opportunities to grow; Emmett Robinson and Norm Weber who taught me the power of language and actions; Annie N. and Anne T. and their encouragement to spread my wings.

Wayne Yenawine who believed in me and gave me a chance; Dr. Charlie Bryant and Dr. John Sattler, who saved my life; for Bill Oglesby and Bill Arnold's insightful encouragement into pastoral care; for Luther Mauney, Bob Young, and Marlyne Cain, who encouraged me to stretch and grow and helped me develop real humility; for the Emergency Department staff at the Medical College of Virginia Hospitals/VCU; for the nurses, clerks, and other staff of the Neuroscience Intensive Care Unit.

Fred and Lori G. and their encouragement to do the work in bereavement and organ, tissue, and eye donation; Bill Proctor;

Acknowledgements

Edward Meeks (Pope) Gregory, and Dr. Elizabeth Reynolds for their love and support; for the MCV Bereavement Committee; Jack Morgan, mentor and friend; Peter Ford, Robert Howell, Gerry Cox, Darcy Harris, Dick Gilbert, Rob Stevenson, and Joy Johnson, who offered me the gift of friendship and inclusion.

Jeannie and Bill and the rich opportunities to laugh and cry; J. B., J. L., D. P. and D. M., from whom I learned a great deal about loving; Kyle and Marla, from and with whom I've celebrated many of life's transitions; Nevada, Jewelie, and Reagan who supported me in my efforts; Elliot B., Fran S., Barbara P., Gwen S., every student I've ever had the joy of teaching, (you taught me much); my friends and colleagues at the Center for Organ Recovery and Education, Arkansas Organ Recovery Agency, and Lifenet.

My sisters-in-law Anne M. and Patty M. who have been models of grace, encouragement, and acceptance; my son Ben, whose gifts and challenges have taught me so much that has helped me help myself and others, and my wife and best friend Laura who has been a part of my life since I was nine-years-old and who has encouraged, cajoled, and nurtured me into becoming and who has been and is truly the wind beneath my sails. For all the churches with which I've had the privilege of ministering and the Presbytery Colleagues; and lastly to Mary Jo R. and Ron L., Derek W., Laurel H., Dick G., Laura F., Joy J. Fran S., and Janine A., who have been my editors, readers, and prompts to do it better. And lastly, to all the other family, friends, colleagues, parishioners, and students whose names are legion, I give you heartfelt thanks for having allowed me into your lives.

Introduction

This book was not supposed to be! My writing of it began as a story written while attending the International Death, Grief, and Bereavement Conference in June of 2013. By the end of the opening plenary session, my mind was racing, filled with a glut of stories.

There was a sense of immediacy in the writing of "Black Ice," one of the stories found in the following pages, as though the details might slip away if not put quickly to paper. Following that story's publication in a grief journal, I had a number of close friends who encouraged me to write more.

As I began writing, the stories gushed out as though they had been contained behind a dam. While all of the stories are true, some of the details have been altered and names changed to protect the anonymity of the individuals and their families.

As I reflected back across the decades of my life, one of the realities that struck me was the fact that during the sexual revolution, sex came out of "the closet," simultaneously forcing death into "the closet." As our society focused more of its energies on sexuality, there seems to have been an ever-increasing withdrawal from death as an active part of life, framing the reality that we have become a more death-avoidant society.

Because language shapes our culture, our language around death influences the way we approach or distance ourselves from it as a part of life: for instance, we talk about people as having

Introduction

"passed," "expired," "bought the farm," "kicked the bucket," or we use a myriad of other euphemisms to talk about a naturally, and occasionally an unnaturally, occurring event. This book explores the reality of death in our lives and exposes the reader to a variety of tragic death accounts. Very few of the deaths or losses in these stories are neat and clean, but in truth they are replete with the capricious nature of death and loss along with its raw and often very graphic and cruel aspects.

In my own life, I find that many of the memories I have are framed by stories of love and loss. This book was written as a memoir of the period beginning when I was 19 years old and first employed in a hospital as a nursing assistant. It follows my changing levels of responsibility and growth as a professional over the course of four decades ending with my last employment as a hospital chaplain in 2009.

My life, and I believe probably the lives of most of us, has been replete with a variety of learning experiences, some intentional and others incidental, but each having a shaping influence on who and what I've become. Many of the incidents about which I have written were events that were a part of my experience at various points along my professional and personal journey.

The majority of the stories were drawn from my time spent as chaplain and coordinator of bereavement services at the Medical College of Virginia Hospitals, a level I trauma center located in downtown Richmond, Virginia. In that role, I was fortunate enough to work with the staff, patients, and families in the Trauma Emergency Room as well as the Neuroscience Intensive Care Unit.

My hope as you read these stories is that you will connect with the patients and families and catch a small glimpse of the variety of experiences that those in healthcare face on a daily basis. I hope it also will provide you a view of the anguish that families encounter as they struggle to make decisions brought on by a healthcare delivery system which wrestles with its part in making death a protracted and often unnatural event. In truth as we, as a society, grapple with how death occurs, each of us will confront

Introduction

many different and unique aspects of death that most of us would just as soon forego as a part of our lives.

With this awareness, I also hope you will find these narratives of benefit as you reflect upon occurrences from your life that have forged, challenged, and infused both meaning and hope into life's journey!

Chapter 1

Too Young

Richard was only 16 when he was first diagnosed with leukemia. The year was 1968, a time of great turmoil in the Deep South as people began to live with the Civil Rights Act of 1964. Why that bears any relevance is that I began working in the hospital in 1969 because of a strike which was going on in Charleston at the time. It was during that experience that I first met Richard.

I had begun my second year in college and needed a way to fund my education, so when the hospital was desperately looking for able bodies to work during the strike, I seized the opportunity. I never dreamed at age 19 that I would be caring for someone who was two years younger than me–and dying!

I must tell you that when I began working as a nursing assistant I didn't know beans about what I was doing. I'd never taken a blood pressure or read a thermometer, and I certainly didn't know how to make a bed or bathe someone. My patients truly were my teachers, along with a host of tolerant and incredibly patient staff members, aides, nurses, medical students, and physicians alike.

I remember Richard's mother and father hovering around Richard's bed in a four-bed male ward. They both appeared to have eyes glazed with gossamer veils, enabling them to focus all of their attention on their frail son and blocking out any other distractions in the room.

Following a blood transfusion or two, Richard would rally and seem like any other now 17-year-old boy with hopes and dreams of a future beyond the existence of a hospital bed. But several days later, as Richard's red blood cells were consumed by his body, Richard was back to where he was prior to the transfusions.

I came and went between school and work with a rich and full social life. My days were punctuated with studying and learning new factors about life and living; while Richard simply struggled to breathe and exist from one moment to the next. His parents began to exhibit a dazed look about them as it became increasingly clear that Richard's disease was winning the battle to claim his very young life. They looked less and less able to cope as the sands of time slipped quickly through their hands and Richard's.

Because his parents hovered over him, I rarely ever had the opportunity to talk just to Richard. His parents, if present, always wanted to keep the conversation light. They were attempting to buoy Richard's spirits by acting as if nothing was wrong, maintaining the polite Southern illusion of "fine thank you, and you?" In reality, I think they were trying to buoy their own spirits by acting as though all was fine.

I remember one evening when Richard, in anger and frustration, snatched the veil from his parents' eyes when he screamed at them that he was dying and would not be around long enough to enjoy any of the insane ideas about which they daily blithered. Richard could read the signs that he was dying. He had sores all over his body from the lack of platelets and red blood cells. He was a mere shell of the young man I'm sure he once was before the ravages of disease destroyed his body.

Richard's fatigue was etched on his face and mirrored the faces of his parents, who were walking ghosts moving through the shadows of daily living. I can remember a meeting between Richard's parents and the medical staff, in hushed tones voicing decisions to discontinue treatment as Richard was not in remission and would die soon anyway. I remember Richard's father in

Too Young

particular very stoically trying to hold himself afloat in a sea of denial as the betrayal of a lonely tear and the quiver of his lips betrayed his internal struggles and utter devastation as he tried to pull himself together to face Richard. Richard's mom simply appeared deflated, like a balloon with a steady leak and the air slowly escaping with no means of reclaiming the loss.

For Richard there would be no code blue, no heroic efforts, simply the hope that he would peacefully slip away . . .

Death under many circumstances is not pretty, and Richard's was no different. Because he had no platelets and was bleeding uncontrollably, he was bleeding from every orifice, and attempts to keep him clean and in fresh sheets were an ongoing challenge. Richard died during the night with the moonlight streaming in upon his bed as his parents, sitting in chairs, slept bent over his bed. A quiet tribute to what might have been.

Chapter 2

A Fish Named Rudolph

Stories that usually are woven into the fabric of our lives are full of both humor and pathos; Sammie's is one of those. Over the years I have probably written and rewritten this story in my mind hundreds of times.

Laura and I married relatively young; she was 20 and I was 21. For those at that age it is difficult to find a place to fit in because you're in that "already but not yet" place of development; while technically an adult, you just don't seem to mesh into the adult world quite yet. Fortunately for us there was a group at our church which allowed us in, even though we were the youngest in the organization; it was known as the Young Scots. One of the "older" couples who were a part of that group was Grace and Steve.

Grace taught school at one of the local Hebrew schools, and Steve was an accountant with one of the local hospitals. Grace had a remarkable sense of humor; Steve was always more of a background presence as the "straight man" to Grace. They had moved to Charleston from Alabama and brought with them their toe-headed 3-year-old by the name of Sammie.

Grace and Steve had married at a later age and decided, prior to Sammie's birth, that Grace would have her tubes tied because

A Fish Named Rudolph

she really did not wish to go through another pregnancy; Sammie was to be a "signed and numbered edition." Truly a one of a kind!

Sammie was one of those cute little kids: old people yearned to pinch his cheeks, and the rest of us just wanted to tousle his hair. Sammie was charming; probably manipulative with his charms but none the less "cute as a button." Sammie began preschool at age 4 and I'm sure charmed the socks off his teachers while simultaneously giving them a real "run for their money."

Like most 4-year-olds, Sammie was fascinated with goldfish and pestered Steve and Grace into getting him one for his birthday, bowl and all. One morning after Sammie left to go to preschool, Grace noted that "Rudolph" the goldfish was floating belly up in his bowl.

Well Grace, knowing that Sammie would be wondering about Rudolph when she picked him up from preschool, fabricated this elaborate story to tell Sammie. So on the ride home from preschool, Grace shared her elaborate story with Sammie about how Rudolph had been lonely and wanted desperately to go and swim with the other fish in the ocean. Sammie, in all of his childhood innocence, flashed a look like, "really, you're thinking I'm buying this truckload of . . ."

Sammie looked with horror at Grace and announced, "So Rudolph died and you flushed him, huh?"

As I heard the story recounted, I'm sure Grace told me she just about ran off the Cooper River Bridge.

Several months later on a Saturday morning, Grace and Steve decided to go furniture shopping; not exactly a 4-year-old's dream trip. They went out Savannah Highway to Them's Furniture Store, having been told that it had a great selection of furniture. As they wandered around in the store for a couple of hours, Sammie became increasingly agitated, so finally Steve took his son to the front parking lot so Sammie could run around and play.

Sammie decided he'd rather wait in the car, so Steve stood on the front steps of Them's to watch him and keep an eye on him as the child crossed the parking lot to the safety of their vehicle. As the cosmic forces aligned themselves, simultaneously there was a vehicle headed toward town with a sad, disturbed man behind the wheel. The man had a substance-abuse problem and was driving under the influence of alcohol.

About the time Sammie was almost safely to the car with Steve watching, a car swerved off the road and careened through the parking lot, striking Sammie and several parked vehicles. To Steve's horror, Sammie lay very still and sort of peacefully on the pavement of the parking lot as his scream hung in the air.

Somehow an ambulance was called, and Sammie's small body was medflighted to the Medical University of South Carolina's trauma room. Sometime during that day, Sammie was declared brain dead and became an organ donor. Much in the same way that Sammie had known about Rudolph, I often wondered whether or not Sammie also knew about his own impending death; a life far too brief, full of love and laughter. A gift given; a gift received. Sammie, may you and Rudolph rest in eternal peace.

Chapter 3

Leather Restraints

Unlike Sammie, Leroy desperately needed a transplant and could have benefited from an organ donor. By the time 1970 rolled around, I was an old hand at my job as a nursing assistant. I'd been doing it for about a year and was becoming comfortable with the medical jargon and even began to understand anatomically something about what-was-connected-to-what.

That summer I met Leroy S., a big African American man in his early 40s, which at the time I thought was quite old. I say big because at our initial meeting Leroy was six-foot-four and probably weighed close to 300 pounds. He reminded me of the actor who played the role of "Big Sam" in the movie *Gone with the Wind*.

Leroy, like so many African Americans, had a problem with hypertension, or high blood pressure. He'd had the problem for about ten years and it had grown progressively worse to the point that he was having kidney problems and was facing the potential for hemodialysis as a bridge to a kidney transplant.

Leroy was one of those unforgettable people, not just because of his size but because he possessed a brightness of spirit which seemed to emanate from his very core. His smile went from ear to ear, and his eyes danced when he was smiling, which was most of the time. He also enjoyed a deep and abiding faith which he used for solace and hope during his illness. While Leroy was content with his faithfulness to the God of his understanding, I was still busy at that time trying to determine the breadth and depth of the God in whom, I believed, or at least thought I wanted to believe.

Leroy was an interesting man, having grown up prior to the 1964 Civil Rights Act. He held a value for education and struggled to make certain that his children received a quality education. At the time I met him, he had a son in school at Moorhead University and a daughter preparing to attend Howard University. Leroy truly was a visionary, far beyond his years.

Kidney transplants were still a rarity, and the overwhelming majority of those were family donations as cadaveric donations were seldom available and the techniques for using cadaveric organs were still in their infancy. Even directed family donations were rare because of the specificity of tissue required for a match which had to be painstakingly exact because of the body's design to reject foreign tissues. Another complicating factor was the very real paucity of beneficial anti-rejection drugs. While many studies explored these challenges at that time, the challenge of graft rejection remained a major consideration in surgery for kidney transplantation.

Additional considerations in whether or not to transplant someone were based upon socio-economics and the patient's ability to pay not only for the transplant, but also for the cost of the medications required to sustain the graft if a matching kidney was transplanted. Another consideration was whether or not the individual had family that would be there to provide emotional support when the journey became tough.

In addition to his role as a part-time Baptist pastor, Leroy worked for the county maintenance shop doing manual labor. But the sicker Leroy became, the less likely he was able to function and maintain the physical demands of his secular employment. Because of the inability to secure a donor match from Leroy's family, the decision was made to remove Leroy from hemodialysis since it was no longer acting as a bridge to transplant.

Leather Restraints

When that decision was made, I believe Leroy and his wife both experienced a real crisis of spirit. Or perhaps that was my own projection. Shortly thereafter Leroy began to decline rapidly. Initially Leroy's wife and children were in constant attendance at his bedside, but as his condition deteriorated, so did the frequency of their visits. As Leroy's blood urea nitrogen (BUN) climbed as a result of the renal failure and the other toxins he could no longer excrete through his diseased kidneys were no longer being removed from his body through hemodialysis, Leroy became more and more confused and combative.

About a week and a half after Leroy was removed from dialysis I went into to work one evening and found Leroy in two-inch leather restraints, thrashing around, hollering, and generally out of his mind. Apparently on the day shift he had "hauled off" and "clobbered" one of my co-workers. As Leroy's BUN continued to rise, so did his level of confusion and agitation.

He reminded me of someone who, twenty years later, might have been hopped up on PCP or some other stimulating illegal drug. His strength was amazing even though he had dropped to 130 pounds. Finally after a week of wrestling with "Samson," Leroy finally slipped into a coma, the restraints were removed, and his wife and children began holding a vigil around his bed until he died a very peaceful death.

I don't know whatever happened to his family. I like to hope that they were able to pick up the pieces of their lives, grieve, and continue living. That was what Leroy told them he wanted them to do: "Make me proud," Leroy said many times to his loved ones who kept vigil.

From Leroy I learned a plethora of life shaping lessons. I learned that while many of our cultural behaviors were different, at the core of our humanity we are all the same, carrying similar hopes and desires for those who follow us as heirs. I also learned that despite his condition, most people die the way they live. Leroy died very quietly in an almost dignified fashion, and I like to envision that was the way he lived his life. Leroy's refrain, "Make me proud" still echoes in the recesses of my mind . . .

Chapter 4

A Book of Poems

Bill and I first met in grammar school when I was in fourth grade and he was in fifth. He was one of those people who "had it all." He was bright, good looking, athletic, and generally multi-talented. In ninth grade he transferred to a different high school, and we lost track of one another, moving in different circles.

It wasn't until we were in our mid-to-late twenties that our paths again crossed. I was on faculty at the University of South Carolina (USC) as a medical librarian, and he was a second-year law student at USC. He came into the medical library to do some research for a paper for his torts class; we spotted each other, and all the years we'd not seen each other dissipated like vapor into thin air.

While we were both a bit older, he at least was still incredibly handsome but now in a more mature body. He was in a rush to make it to his next class but said he'd be back so we could catch up. In our brief encounter Bill's intensity was palpable, and I found myself wondering about its origins.

Bill showed up about a week later, and we visited for a long time. He had been living in Columbia, South Carolina for several years. He had taught grammar school prior to attending law school, but decided that was not what he wanted to do for the rest of his life.

Bill joined Laura and me for dinner, and the three of us had a great time together. We laughed and reminisced about Charleston and its idiosyncrasies, and it was then that Bill shared with us that he was a gay man and was very lonely. We told Bill about another friend of ours who was in a similar situation and shortly thereafter introduced the two of them to one another.

Bill and Henry became fast friends and could be found on occasion out shopping or doing any number of activities together, but even in those times of seeming delight there were tangible traces of an underlying core of sadness. The four of us would frequently share a meal together, and, as the school year progressed, I would usually see Bill at least once a week when he would come to the library just to visit.

I think Bill had sort of adopted Laura and me as family since, like us, his family of origin all lived in Charleston. He never mentioned them, which always left me wondering whether he had severed ties with them—or they with him, because of who he was.

Bill came to see me at the library about two months into his final year of law school. He seemed more frenetic and bizarre than I'd previously experienced him, which made me wonder if he was unraveling emotionally. One day he came in and told me he had something he wanted to give me. He said it was a book of his poetry that he'd been writing and wanted me to have.

He came in about two days later and dropped it off, rambling somewhat incoherently. Initially I was very touched that he would impart such a personal gift to me, but after he left I opened the book and began to read what seemed to me to be sheer gibberish and nonsense, causing the hairs on my neck to bristle with angst.

Laura and I talked about the book that night, wondering what to do about it. We both speculated about Bill's motives for giving it to me. Was he suicidal, and was this a final gesture? Was he mentally unstable and crying out for help?

A couple of days passed, and I saw nothing of Bill, nor could I reach him by phone. On the third day I received a phone call in the morning prior to leaving for work; it was Bill's roommate–someone I'd never met. He was calling to tell me that he'd found Bill's body that morning with a self-inflicted gunshot wound to the head. My name and phone number were on a list of people to notify that Bill had left.

I was dumbstruck and devastated. I couldn't believe what I was hearing. I knew that something wasn't right from the book of "poetry" he had given me, but somehow I never expected this. I felt cheated. I felt robbed. I felt devastated and sad.

After all of the years we'd not seen each other to simply "off" himself with no words of farewell–how dare HE! About a week after Bill's death, I received a phone call from his understandably distraught mother. During our brief conversation she asked whether I knew anything about what had happened to her dear son. I explained to her about the book of "poetry" with which I'd been "gifted."

Then came her impugning words of indictment: "You knew something wasn't right and you did nothing?" Oh my God, had I really known about Bill's journey toward killing himself and done nothing? My thoughts became somewhat blurred. How could I have let him down in this way? Did I not care? Was his life so cheap?

I've pondered those questions for almost forty years. In reflecting on the events of those days, I've mentally replayed them thousands of times. What I've told myself is that I was young and that I did the best I was able to do given the nature of the situation and my own development and education about suicide. God knows I wish I known/done more. I also figured out along my life's journey that his mother was absolutely devastated and was lashing out in her unrequited grief.

I'll always remember Bill, who was perhaps too sensitive and kind a man to survive in the world in which we live . . . You'll always be a part of me Bill; I still miss you as a presence in my life . . .

Chapter 5

A Babysitter

The level to which brokenness is rampant within the human race never ceases to amaze me! As I began my Clinical Pastoral Education residency I was taking in-house calls, and on my first night on duty there was a trauma team alert around 10 in the evening. A 2-year-old was brought in by ambulance with CPR in progress. The stretcher was followed immediately by two distraught people whom I came to know as Aven's parents, Michelle and Devon.

As we sat together in the family conference room, I listened as they told me and the city police officer what had happened. Initially within my head I thought this must be a SIDS (sudden infant death syndrome) death. But as the story unfolded, it was anything but!

Michelle and Devon had waited for several years after their marriage to have children. Aven was their first, and they loved him with all their hearts. Aven had just recently turned 2, and like most toddlers that age he was full of energy and headstrong with a determination to say "no" as often as possible.

Devon had a reception to attend for work that particular evening, and Michelle was able to attend with him, having secured the services of a babysitter for the evening. Thinking that they would make a night of it, Devon made arrangements to take Michelle out to dinner prior to attending the reception. They truly were dedicated parents and in fact had chosen for Michelle to be a stay-at-home mom with Aven, at least until he began first grade.

The babysitter Michelle secured for the evening had been used by some friends of theirs, so they felt relatively comfortable as they set out for their evening of freedom from the momentary responsibilities of caring for Aven. Their dinner was great and the reception was, as many work receptions are, interesting but not a place one would chose to spend the overwhelming majority of one's daily life, so they said! Following the reception, Michelle and Devon returned home.

The babysitter greeted them at the door upon their arrival and told them what a sweet child Aven had been. The sitter indicated that Aven had taken a tumble down the stairs and had been tired and so he had gone ahead and put Aven in bed about 6:30 p.m. It was a little early for Aven to retire, but neither Michelle nor Devon thought much about it. After all, 2-year-olds are notorious for taking tumbles and being somewhat erratic in their sleeping patterns.

Devon paid the sitter who took his leave, and he and Michelle went upstairs to check on Aven and to get ready for bed, as it had been a long day and evening. A nightlight was on in Aven's room, so they could go in and check on him without the concern of accidentally awakening him.

When they went in they were aware of the sweet odor of baby and smiled at each other as they walked over to Aven's crib. When they went to pull the blanket up on Aven they noticed some blood on the sheets, which caused immediate alarm. They rolled Aven over on his back as he was on his stomach, and both of them about wretched when they saw his bruised face, wondering exactly what had happened.

They called the sitter, and he assured them that he had no idea what could have happened aside from the fall down the steps, which he'd already told them about. In my head I was thinking this is clearly a case of child abuse of some sort, and as a mandated

A Babysitter

reporter I knew I needed to call the child abuse hotline. I found myself wondering as I listened to the parents' story just where the truth lay.

Michelle and Devon proceeded with their story, and I, who am usually very empathic, became more and more suspicious about what had transpired. The police officer did too as he radioed in and asked for a forensic unit to be dispatched to the home of Michelle and Devon with their consent to try to determine what might have occurred.

Michelle and Devon continued: They said that they immediately picked Aven up and began to assess his little body for additional damage. They said that he was very listless and unresponsive, and they noted bruising on his body too. As they completed their story, the pediatric attending physician came in to tell them that Aven had died, apparently from blunt trauma. Michelle and Devon sat there with unbelieving faces and denial upon their lips.

"No, this can't be, there must be some mistake." Each was . . . looking from one person's face to the next to see if someone was perhaps playing a very cruel joke on them. "He was just fine when we left him this evening. He can't be dead."

Tears and raspy breathing caught in their throats as one of the city detectives arrived and began questioning Michelle and Devon, leaving no room for grieving the death of their toddler son. I'm certain they were looking for holes in Michelle and Devon's story. Simultaneously they must have obtained information about the babysitter and gone to have a talk with the sitter as well.

It wasn't much later that another detective arrived to inform Michelle and Devon that they had taken the babysitter into custody and he had confessed to having thrown Aven down the stairs in a fit of rage because Aven kept crying. How could something so "right" have gone so terribly awry?

A child's life snuffed out and two parents left to carry the burden that maybe at some level they bore culpability for his death. After all, it is the responsibility of all parents to protect their children. Devon and Michelle had failed! Two lives were now trapped

Through the Eyes of the Heart

in a web of permanent despair. Three lives were destroyed in a fit of rage. Tell me brokenness doesn't abound!

Chapter 6

Pizza Delivery

One evening while doing my chaplaincy residency, I was on call and received a page from the registration clerk in the Emergency Department of the Medical College of Virginia Hospitals telling me that they had just placed a man in the family conference room and could I come down and see him. I assured them that I would be right down as it had been a rather quiet night so far, and I was glad to have something to do to break up what portended to be a long night of walking the halls.

When I arrived at the conference room there sat an older gentleman, probably in his mid-60s. He was on the phone, so I waited in the hallway until he finished. I went in and introduced myself as the duty chaplain, and I asked what I could do to help. He explained that he had received a call from someone that his grandson Joseph had been injured on the job and was being brought to MCV for treatment.

I must have looked a little bit surprised because I hadn't heard about any traumas being brought in, so I thought perhaps his grandson had been brought in as a regular patient but wasn't serious enough to warrant activating a trauma team alert.

We talked for several minutes as I gathered information about his grandson. He told me that Joseph was much more like a son to him. He explained that when Joseph was about 8 his father had killed his mother, and he had been jailed to serve a twenty-year sentence for first-degree murder, so Joseph had come to live with his grandfather at that time.

He told me that Joseph had turned out to be a really fine young man. He said that Joseph was a good student and now at age 16 had taken an after-school job delivering pizza. He said that he wasn't thrilled about the type of job Joseph had but that Joseph had talked him into allowing him to take the job, assuring him that he would keep up his grades and his extracurricular activities at school.

Armed with Joseph's full name and birthdate, I excused myself to try and to locate his grandson. I checked with registration, and they had no one who had been admitted that afternoon or evening fitting the boy's description. I walked through the Emergency Department just to make certain they hadn't missed someone, and then I went back to tell his grandfather that we didn't have his grandson as a patient.

With a rather stunned and incredulous look, he said, "I know they told me that he would be brought here." I said well, occasionally family will get here prior to the ambulance, so I told him he was welcome to wait in the conference room and that I would let him know if Joseph arrived. So after getting him some coffee I went in to check with the triage nurse who said that they had not received any calls about anyone fitting Joseph's description being brought in to the Emergency Room.

After about twenty minutes of waiting, expecting to hear something, I went back in to see Joseph's grandfather and to find out what ambulance service he thought might be transporting Joseph. He looked at me rather curiously and seemed momentarily disoriented. He shared that Joseph was working in Hanover County. Having garnered that little snippet of information, I began my investigative work with tingles running up and down my spine, beginning to believe that all was not as it seemed.

After calling the Hanover Sheriff's Department and gaining no assistance, I called the Richmond Police Department. I

Pizza Delivery

explained to the officer who I was and why I was calling. He told me that a young man fitting Joseph's description had been delivering pizza in a rather "shady" area of town and had been shot in the head and robbed. Now armed with that bit of information, I experienced a sick feeling in the pit of my stomach. I asked the officer to please confirm the identity of the victim and to call me back.

Reluctantly, I went back in to share with the grandfather that I was waiting for the Richmond Police Department to call me back. He smiled a rather contemplative smile as he continued to talk about the joy he'd had in raising Joseph. He told me that his wife had died two years before of cervical cancer and that Joseph had helped him make it through that very difficult and tragic death, again reiterating what a fine young man Joseph had become.

About twenty minutes passed, and I finally received a phone call from the investigating detective confirming my worst fears. Heartsick, I went in to share with Joseph's grandfather that Joseph had been robbed and for the amount of $8.21 he had been killed. His body had been taken directly to the medical examiner's office for an autopsy.

He wept out loud, my hand resting upon his shoulder! I wept inwardly for his loss and the sadness of such a promising young life cut short. I walked him to his car where we hugged, and he rode into the dark night, alone once again . . .

Chapter 7

One of Our Own

While serving my residency in Clinical Pastoral Education (CPE), there were many remarkable experiences. This event happened immediately following my residency as I was transitioning to being a faculty member in the Department of Pastoral Care and would shape the rest of my time working with the Emergency Department staff.

Because my position had been partially funded by the transplant teams, it was determined that two areas of foci for my work would need to be both the Neuroscience Intensive Care Unit and the Emergency Department since both of those areas held the greatest likelihood for producing potential organ, tissue, and eye donors.

The premise behind the funding of my faculty appointment was that if we cared for families at the initial points of contact with a consistent presence, the likelihood of families donating would increase. Obviously I couldn't cover twenty-four hours a day and so our CPE residents and interns were instructed in the best approaches to assist families when I was unavailable, such as on the weekends.

As it happened, my wife Laura was doing an internship in CPE at the same time I was transitioning into my new role and

One of Our Own

was the chaplain on call when this particular patient was brought in from an automobile crash. When Laura arrived for this trauma team alert, it was no different from arriving for any other traumatic event. Everyone was a bit edgy with the awareness that the condition of the patient could deteriorate and their potential survival could get rather dicey very quickly once the unknown rolled through the doors.

The word that was received prior to the arrival of the ambulance crew was that they were bringing in a woman who was very unstable and in all likelihood had sustained a severe brain injury from a crash scene. When there was suspected brain involvement, the neurosurgery resident was paged to be present in the Emergency Department to assess the extent of likely brain damage.

This particular patient had sustained numerous fractures in addition to the head trauma, so she was a bloody mess upon arrival. As any well-oiled machine runs, everyone on the trauma team has a job to do, knows their job, and carries it off with great efficacy and dispatch.

The neurosurgery resident sent the patient immediately to cat scan to assess the depth and breadth of the brain injury, whereupon it was determined that her other injuries were secondary in importance and that to provide her the greatest likelihood of any meaningful recovery she was moved hastily to the Neuroscience Intensive Care Unit (NSICU). It wasn't until later as the nurses in the ICU were cleaning off some of the blood that they realized that this was a nurse whom they knew. Not only was she a nurse they knew, but she was someone with whom many of them had worked very closely.

The nurse's name was Shauna. Shauna had worked in the Emergency Department (ED) as part of the nursing management team and had been on maternity leave, having given birth to a beautiful baby boy after which she and her husband had separated. In addition to her work in the ED, Shauna had been training to work part-time in the NSICU, so staffs in both areas of the hospital were in real turmoil when she was identified.

Through the Eyes of the Heart

By the time I was notified and arrived on Monday morning, grieving individuals were all over the hospital. Some in the ED were feeling guilty because they hadn't recognized Shauna even though they had worked closely together, many for eight years or more.

It's one, difficult enough to care for "strangers," it is a totally different experience when it is "one of our own," pointing toward our very real vulnerability to needing care as well. All I could do was provide a listening ear and a shoulder upon which to cry. I heard numerous replays of the event by staff as each in his or her own way was trying to make some sense out of this awful situation. I also offered a sort of "absolution" for those who were feeling a sense of guilt about not knowing who it was they were working on so efficiently.

Mid-morning on that traumatic Monday family began arriving for Shauna, and my focus had to shift from being a supportive colleague and chaplain to the staff to being chaplain to a devastated and frightened family. There was Shauna's estranged husband Jimmy, a firefighter whom I knew from his visits to the ED with other patients. There were also Shauna's parents, who were very worried about their daughter and not particularly thrilled to be in the same space with Jimmy.

Because there was no legal separation in place, Jimmy was the legal decision-maker and primary parent for his young son. To Shauna's parents' credit they made every effort to be as accommodating to Jimmy as they could. I actually saw some real healing of old wounds as together they worked as a family for Shauna's benefit.

Two weeks into this nightmare it was determined that while Shauna might survive this event, there was great concern about her quality of life. Shauna, like many of us, always had been very clear about the fact that she would not wish to survive if she was not fully functional and able to enjoy the rich and full life for which she held such value.

Jimmy, along with Shauna's parents, and with great heaviness of heart, made the decision to withdraw mechanical supports and to allow Sharon to die a peaceful death. Those two weeks were agonizing because each staff member felt a need to weigh in on what his or her thoughts were relative to Shauna's survival as well as to talk about Jimmy's absence in Shauna's life during her pregnancy and now having full custody of a child he initially didn't seem to have wanted.

But somehow during those weeks most everyone moved to a place of greater ease. Jimmy and his son found themselves embraced and enfolded as family by the ED staff, not an easy group with whom to find one's place of acceptance.

I rarely agreed to be a part of a funeral, but for this one, since I was asked by Shauna's family and also was strongly encouraged by the ED staff, I did take part in the service. As sad as it was, Shauna's death cemented my relationship with the ED staff. Following Shauna's death, Jimmy would periodically show up at my office to tell me how he and his son were doing. Jimmy had gone back to school and had developed a real sense of purpose for his life, which had been a big part of the reason he and Shauna had separated.

Life takes interesting turns.

Chapter 8

Alone

Emily was 9 years old with dark hair and beautiful hazel eyes. In some ways she seemed much younger than her years would indicate, but when you live like Emily did, I think there is probably a tendency to try to remain unscathed, childlike, in a safe place, at least emotionally. Her clothes were blood spattered, attesting to the fact that something awful must have occurred in her presence.

The morning I met Emily was like most mornings except for the circumstances that brought our lives into overlap. I had begun my morning as usual at the Medical College of Virginia Hospitals; I first attended morning report, during which the night-duty chaplain would apprise us of the shift's activities, following which I went by my office to drop off my belongings and prepare to begin a new day.

As I came out of my office I noticed Emily sitting on the floor in the intensive care unit waiting room, apparently alone. I walked in and sat down on the floor and introduced myself to her. Since we usually discouraged anyone under the age of 12 from being on that floor because of the risk of harm to them due to the assaults upon their young and underdeveloped immune systems, I was really puzzled as to why she was there with no apparent supervision.

Alone

What she told me in a very matter-of-fact manner was that her mother was in the Neuroscience Intensive Care Unit and that she was waiting for her grandmother to come and stay with her. As I probed and asked her what happened to her mommy she said that her daddy had shot her mommy in the head and then turned the gun on himself, killing himself.

"Where were you?" I naively asked when this all happened, assuming that she might have been in her bed asleep or getting dressed for school. She looked at me with quivering lips and eyes brimming with tears and said, "I was hitting my daddy telling him to leave my mommy alone."

... I think I went into one of those momentary blackouts. In my own head I was thinking that explained the blood spattered shirt!

While I was trying to comprehend what I'd heard, Emily continued, "Now that my daddy is dead and my mommy is dying, who is going to take care of me?"

I felt tightness in my chest as I heard her question asked.

"I don't know honey, we'll have to wait and talk that over with your grandmother when she gets here."

I desperately needed to breathe for a moment as my own fears of abandonment gripped me (when I was 13 my mother who was my custodial parent had open-heart surgery, one of the first in the nation and the risk was very great that she would die,) I needed an opportunity to regroup the troops. So I asked Emily if she had had any breakfast, and when she answered no, I stood up and said, "Let me go see what I can find in the NSICU, and I'll be right back."

I walked to the unit with real purpose to my steps playing the scene from *Forrest Gump* in my own mind when his girlfriend hollered at him, "Run Forrest, run;" exactly what I felt like doing.

I walked into the unit and immediately went to find Monique, the nurse caring for Emily's mom, to get the story on what was going on and to find out how Emily's mom was doing.

Monique told me that LifeNet had already been contacted and that they were on their way in to assess Emily's mom as a potential organ donor since her injuries were non-survivable. In my head all I could think was, Oh my God, this child was a witness to and a part of her father killing her mother and then killing himself. How as a child do you even begin to recover or make sense from something like this?"

I tried to get myself together as I knew I had a tough day ahead, trying to help a 9-year-old understand that not only was her dad dead, but so was her mom!

Knowing that children are usually very concrete in their thinking at this age and that she was still only a 9-year-old even though she had been thrust into an adult role, I contacted the child life specialist to determine if there were some suitable materials for Emily to play with since children frequently express their grief through play. I also obtained some cereal and milk, all that was available on the unit, and I dashed up to pediatrics and retrieved some drawing paper and crayons along with some Play-Doh and a stuffed animal and went back downstairs to join Emily. I had commandeered one of the conference rooms near the NSICU so that she could be in a more private place and closer to her mom upon her grandmother's arrival.

I asked Emily what she understood about her mother's condition. She told me that when the police had come to their house, she had heard them say that her mommy was dead too; a murder/suicide. I asked Emily what that meant to her and that was when she once again asked the question, "What's going to happen to me now that my parents are dead?"

Echoing it tore at the strings of my heart!

As children often will do, throughout the morning, Emily would color some and then play make believe with the stuffed animals I'd garnered for her.

At about 11 a.m. Emily's grandmother finally arrived in a breathless dither. The police had contacted her and told her what had happened, and while she was distraught, she was also trying hard to hold it together. I'm not sure whether she was doing that to protect Emily or herself, but none the less, she was relatively calm, all things considered.

Alone

The medical examiner's office had agreed to allow Emily's mother to be an organ donor as long as the grandmother consented to the donation.

As Emily's grandmother talked, I learned that she had traveled from Virginia Beach, a good two-hour drive from Richmond. I'm not sure exactly what I was expecting or hoping for in a grandmother for Emily, but I can tell you that the woman who arrived did not fit my hoped-for image.

She appeared to be maybe in her early 60s with dyed jet-black hair, overdone makeup, and clothes which fit her much too tightly. In my way of thinking at the time, she looked like an aged hooker, hardly a grandmother. She was the quintessential image of poor white trailer trash. Obviously, at least in my head, my value judgments were running wild. Grandmother's name was Maudy, and while she looked the way she did, she actually had a really tender heart and was able to embrace Emily, grieve with her, and assure her that she did indeed have someone who would love and care for her.

Upon receiving that reassurance from Maudy, Emily drifted across the room once again to color a picture for her grandmother, and Maudy and I had a chance to talk. Maudy indicated a willingness to speak with the people who were there to provide her with options from Lifenet.

As time progressed, Dr. B came in to share with Maudy that Bridgette, her daughter, had been declared dead. Maudy took some time to take in the news and to say what a rotten son of a bitch her son-in-law and the father of Emily had been. She allowed herself to break down and cry only once and quickly pulled herself together, knowing that Emily was watching and not wanting to frighten her. I assured her that it was okay for her to cry because in doing so it would grant Emily unspoken permission to cry as well, but old behaviors die hard.

She asked if they could go in and see Bridgette's body. I assured her that they most certainly could. I asked if the folks there to offer options could come in and speak with her prior to their going in to say their goodbyes.

Having assured me that it was okay, I introduced Denise, the coordinator from LifeNet. Denise was very kind to Maudy and to Emily as they discussed the option of organ, tissue, and eye donation. Maudy and Bridgette had previously had a conversation about organ donation, so it was a pretty easy decision for Maudy to make since Bridgette had a friend who was waiting for a kidney transplant and who had been on dialysis for almost a year while waiting and praying for a kidney.

Maudy asked important questions of Denise about disfigurement of Bridgette's body and was assured that in a casket Bridgette's body would appear no different, but that they might want to plan for her to wear a high-necked blouse since they would make a long incision in her chest and belly to be able to recover the organs.

After Denise finished the consent process for organ donation, Maudy again asked if they could see Bridgette. Absolutely, but I told them that before we went in I'd like to explain first what they were going to see.

I explained to both of them that Bridgette's body was still connected to mechanical supports, which made it appear that Bridgette's body was still alive, but that her brain, the computer that runs the body, had in fact been destroyed by the bullet. I explained that there were still a host of monitors at Bridgette's bedside so that there might be some beeping and buzzing and that these would all remain there until Bridgette's body was taken to the operating room for the organ and tissue recovery.

During this conversation, I could tell that Emily was listening/playing the whole time. She would come over and sort of snuggle into Maudy's embrace, and her grandmother would lovingly return her embrace and kiss her on the top of her head. The image that it conjured for me was that of the famous Madonna and Child.

I continued to feel reassured that as long as Maudy was capable, Emily would receive the love and nurturing she both needed and deserved. Emily colored a landscape overarched by a rainbow with stick figures of her and her mother holding hands on a shore as the sun set across the water.

Alone

As we went in together to say goodbye to Bridgette, Emily stood on tiptoe and reached across Bridgette's body to give her mother a hug and a kiss. Such a tender act from someone so young; Monique, Denise, and I all had tears silently slipping down our cheeks as we watched this final act. Emily tucked her drawing under her mother's arm, and together she and Maudy walked out of the unit to begin their new life together. Emily indeed had found her caregiver.

Chapter 9

Blind

Ralph had been blind since birth—a freak of nature! As a blind child, he had gone to the school for the blind and later attended university. As with many people blind from birth, he had grown up in a sheltered workshop, learning to do all of the task that blind people need to know to exist in a sighted world. He could read braille fluently and loved to listen to books on tape.

Ralph and Kathy met one summer during high school and married when he was 40 and she was 43. They had many discussions about his blindness and the ways in which it might affect their marriage. When I met Ralph, he and Kathy had been married for fourteen years, the last few of which had been pretty rocky.

Shortly after they married Kathy had an unplanned pregnancy. I say unplanned because they had many conversations about the fact that Ralph did not wish to father any children, afraid that his blindness might be genetically linked. When Kathy conceived they were both anxious and concerned.

In the sixth month of her pregnancy, Kathy miscarried. She was devastated; Ralph was grateful, but saddened. Shortly after the termination of the pregnancy, Kathy was diagnosed with a post-partum depression. She began experiencing terrible bouts of depression, coupled with some psychotic episodes.

Blind

Ralph, who had been fairly dependent upon Kathy for both emotional and physical support, was thrust into a position of needing to care for Kathy in ways for which he'd never been schooled. Kathy's depression progressively worsened, and within two years she was routinely receiving electro-shock therapy in addition to her regular medications for depression.

Ralph did not drive for obvious reasons, and Kathy gave up driving, complicating life even further for them both. Kathy was hospitalized numerous times during the next twelve years for her depression and became actively suicidal, attempting to kill herself in a variety of ways and on numerous occasions.

On this particular hospital admission, however, Kathy was not hospitalized for her depression but was in fact hospitalized to deal with some gynecological issues related to menopause that required her to have a D&C (dilation and curettage). Because Ralph was dependent upon public transportation to get around, there were some days that he missed visiting Kathy in the hospital. Kathy often had been a patient at MCV hospitals, so she became fairly comfortable with the myriad of buildings all joined together by various hallways and catwalks, and she learned to navigate the maze fairly effectively.

Hospitals have all kinds of codes that are announced for a variety of causes; for instance, Code Blue is for cardiac arrest, Code Red is for a fire, etc. One afternoon a Code Yellow was announced–not a code for which I had any initial understanding and, in fact, I had to ask several people to find out its meaning. I was informed that it meant that a patient had "eloped" and could not be found.

The call had originated from one of the OB/GYN units, and so I really didn't think much about it until I received a trauma page about forty-five minutes later. When I arrived in the trauma room, cardiopulmonary resuscitation was in progress on a woman who was probably in her mid-to late-50s. As I began to coax the story out of the first responders, I found out it was Kathy who had eloped.

Through the Eyes of the Heart

The word eloped certainly possesses a variety of meanings, but in this case it was used to mean, had disappeared or left a defined area.

As the first responders understood, even though Kathy had been on suicide precautions, she had walked off the unit and gone around to North Hospital, where she located an open window on the ninth floor and jumped into a construction site below. While we were talking they ceased the code on her and declared her time of death.

As I was the chaplain present, it was decided that I should be the one to meet and speak with Ralph about his wife's death. I called him to alert him that he probably needed to come to the hospital, that Kathy had had some complications arise and that she had taken a turn for the worse–a euphemism frequently used when one's physical decline has been determined and death is the likely outcome.

After I hung up the phone from speaking with Ralph, I spent some time talking with the nurse who had been responsible for Kathy's care earlier in the day on the OB/GYN unit. The nurse was upset, to say the very least. She told me about Ralph's blindness and the fact that he didn't drive; when the nursing administrator heard this, the decision made was that I should go and pick up Ralph at his home and bring him to the hospital. I called Ralph back and informed him that I would be leaving to pick him up since it was my understanding from the nurse that he did not drive.

To say I was anxious about doing this was a bit of an understatement! For all I knew Ralph might be a pretty volatile man and might go off on me. Even though I'd dealt frequently with family members whose loved ones had died in the Emergency Department, being removed from my familiar surroundings made me feel somewhat exposed and very vulnerable. I was glad Ralph was blind and could not visibly see my responses and expressions.

Ralph was sitting on the front steps of their home when I drove up and introduced myself to him, leaving out the part that I was one of the hospital chaplains. Ralph was actually a very laid-back man with whom I felt an almost immediate sense of

Blind

connection. He began telling me about Kathy and their long-term challenges with her depression. My tension level began to drop as he shared the fact that Kathy had attempted suicide many times in the past and that he anticipated that one of these times she was going to complete what she heretofore only had attempted.

As I listened to Ralph tell their story, I had tears streaming down my cheeks. I think my tears came from being touched by his level of profound sadness over Kathy's desire to die and the challenges of daily living.

I think another part of Kathy's story that touched me deeply was remembering back to times as an adolescent when I wrestled with the idea of suicide. I can remember sitting on a branch over the Intracoastal Waterway, truly believing in my heart that the world would be a better place without me in it. I guess I'd been feeling sorry for myself and, hearing Ralph talk, I felt pretty foolish.

When we arrived at the hospital, I took Ralph into the Emergency Department's family conference room and offered him water or coffee as I went to see if I could find one of the attending physicians to come in and tell Ralph what had happened to Kathy. The director of risk management also was hovering around, telling me what to say and what not to say so that the hospital could lessen its financial vulnerability. The hospital viewed its liability in this situation to be immense, and management wanted to do everything it could to minimize its potential risk.

I felt like I was caught in the middle of a game of tug-of-war.

When the Emergency Room physician came in to explain to Ralph what had happened to Kathy, Ralph burst into tears and began sobbing. His worst fears had been realized. He cried and as I sat with my arm around his shoulders, I could feel my own sobs of empathy well up from my gut and catch in my throat.

After about thirty minutes of agonizing tears, Ralph began to pull himself together and ask questions about what needed to happen next. I explained to him that because of the nature of Kathy's death, the medical examiner's office already had come to get Kathy's body and that they would be doing an autopsy to make certain there was no foul play involved in her death.

Ralph seemed to take in all of the information calmly and seemed even somewhat resigned to his fate or perhaps excepting of what was. He spoke about Kathy's extreme sadness and ventured that he believed this might have been a real blessing for her to have finally found some sense of peace in an otherwise agonizing and troubling life.

Ralph, after deciding on a funeral home, asked to be taken home. He insisted that he could get a cab while the hospital administrator kept signaling to me that I needed to drive him home, so, twice in one day, I stepped out of my comfort zone and drove Ralph home. I never saw Ralph again after that day's journey together, but I felt a real sense of connectedness with him. As I dropped him off, we stood together and hugged, and I believe I was given the gift of assurance that life is good even in the midst of challenges.

Chapter 10

Black Ice

Bob Niemeyer recently did a presentation at the International Death Grief and Bereavement Conference, and for whatever crazy reason, something he said triggered memories of a death I had been a part of as a chaplain a number of years before. Odd how things happen! This particular time my creative muse decided to work overtime and descended not like a gentle dove but like an anvil. I began writing feverishly, and so here is "Michael's story, a life remembered," as I wrote it several years ago.

A soft drizzle fell upon already cold roads in a rural area near Richmond, Virginia; roads were washed clean and slick as a piece of satin which slides around on a smooth table top, making it just as difficult to control as mercury rolling around on a plate, going first this way and then that. The sky was ominous with the threat of winter weather, which portended a rather bleak and dreary day.

As morning broke, a car left home, headed on its ritualized journey to deliver Michael to school; a boy full of life; mischievous, loving, and full of the joy and wonder of life and learning; eight years of wonder and awe enfolded in an all-boy body full of the hopes and dreams of many tomorrows to come, oblivious to the passage of time and its tolls along the way.

Through the Eyes of the Heart

The car, guided by a loving mother, carrying the fruit of her womb to a place of learning and exploration; the fruit, now grown rich through several years of development; the process of aging and growing richer from life's experiences, encapsulated in his small body, much like a fine wine or a piece of sharp cheese cured and grown more mellow with the passage of time.

Black ice coated the country road which wound toward the elementary school where Michael, a third-grader, would begin yet another day of learning the early lessons of life. A stop sign at the base of a hill; a road covered by a thin sheet of ice. The car which transported this precious cargo attempted to stop but slid into an intersection: stop sign, a sign of caution, a sign of unending horror, a sign of immense challenges to come.

An eighteen-wheeler traveling to unload its cargo and continue its repetitive process of pick up and drop off; a cycle of boredom; a routine of mind-numbing activity.

The car carrying Michael braked and slid; the truck braked and slid, dancing a pas de deux, engaged in a tangle of metal. Michael, who was seat belted in the backseat, with horror viewed the approaching truck. Wham! coup-contra coup–a– movement causing back and forth motion of the brain within the skull); a whirling mass of cold steel, unrelenting, unavoidable, undeniable.

A mother watched in disbelief and heard a scream of eerie, piercing, soul-shattering horror. A cry of anticipated agony escaped her lips as the car spun in a sickening rotation, sliding on cold ice now forever like broken glass.

Deafening silence hung in the air as a confusing haze descended over the metal skeletons of what once was. As awareness dawned a moan escaped a mother's lips as the reality of a broken leg crept up into her morass of consciousness.

The deadly silence now was punctuated only by the awareness of no sound from the backseat. A "brief candle" with only a glowing wick and a mother's hope for rekindling; sirens heard in the distance and a brief attentiveness to all of the movements, sounds, and smells of things present. A tube for breathing with a black balloon attached was the only piece of equipment which stole the illusion of death from Michael's beautiful, unmarred body. The morning's silent, cold air complete with the rhythmic thumping of a helicopter's propellers.

A brief flight; the whir of a cold CT scan delivered a message of despair; the message that this beautiful young boy could no longer benefit from all the high-tech-interventions hovering around his small fragile body. A question hung in the air: what now? A brief exam by the neurosurgeon, followed by a comment inferring that Michael was now in need of only God's "care."

A quick move to the Pediatric Intensive Care Unit, where the cadenced breathing initiated by the ventilator could be heard above the din of usual activity; the tools for determining brain death present at Michael's bedside; ice water, a cotton tipped swab, a syringe and setup for drawing blood gases. Lastly, a physician's declaration of brain death distorted the dreams of what might have been.

Time ticked on, minutes running into hours; a brief trip with the physician to disclose "the death" to a waiting mother whose leg was now cast; shattered hopes and shattered dreams. A mother who had been updated repeatedly throughout the day of how things were going seemed to know before she was told that her beloved son had died. A mother's intuition, I guess!

A wait for the arrival of the designated requestor from the Organ Procurement Agency. A discussion with Mom about the potential for organ donation and a listing of all of the potential gifts that Michael's body could provide. A mass of paperwork to be completed and a trip in a wheelchair to say her goodbyes at Michael's bedside . . . Unwept tears flooding the sheets as a Bear Hugger blew warm air to maintain a body temperature in an already cold and lifeless body. How does one say goodbye to a child one bore and raised to be a youth? How do you begin to discharge the responsibilities of parenting and being there to protect your children from unnamed exposures to harm? How do you initiate the process of closing a relationship of love? The love of a mother for her child and the love of a child for his mother; the guardian charged with comfort, support, and encouragement. A child who in life's journey was seasoned well with acts of generosity of spirit: now in one final scene played out upon the stage of this life . . .

A year later, a chance encounter–or maybe not since there really are no coincidences–at a Celebration for Life event to honor all donor families and to acknowledge the gratitude of recipients for the gift of life so generously given. Who should I stumble upon? Michael's Mother, now married and very much pregnant. During a walk together to meet the recipient of Michael's heart, Michael's mother and I shared tears as we remembered Michael and his brief life lived well. The circle of life complete!

Chapter 11

A Granddame

Mary Margaret Bennett Ravenel had been bestowed with the nickname of Minnie as a young child. Up until that time, she had been called Mary Margaret, a strong Southern name, and for a young woman growing up in the aristocratic South, Mary Margaret was most fitting. Minnie, while sounding somewhat diminutive, seemed to be the name that stuck like glue to her throughout the rest of her life.

But make no mistake; Minnie was in no way diminutive. True enough, she only stood five-feet-two-inches tall and was slight of build; however, she was a big person imbued with lots of pluck. Minnie was educated in the finest Southern girls' schools in Richmond, Virginia and completed her education as a Southern belle at Agnes Scot another fine women's school located near Atlanta.

It was while she was a student there that Minnie first met the love of her life, Josiah Cornelius Bell Ravenel III, who was completing a residency in family medicine at Emory in Decatur, Georgia. Joe was from Charleston, South Carolina, and had attended medical school at the Medical College of South Carolina, later to become known as the Medical University of South Carolina.

After a rather whirlwind courtship, Joe and Minnie decided to marry. Minnie's father was most distressed but agreed that they could marry, depending upon Joe's willingness to relocate and establish his medical practice in Richmond, the former capitol of the Confederacy. A bit outdated as a notion, but characteristic of thinking at that time.

Joe and Minnie were married at St. Paul's Episcopal Church across and down the street from the State Capitol of Virginia. They married in 1933 and were happily married for thirty-five years. While Joe enjoyed a vibrant and active practice in Richmond, Minnie was busy miscarrying eight pregnancies and carrying one child to term, a son who lived until the age of 17 and was taken in the polio epidemic in the 1940s.

Minnie was one of those people who, despite the personal tragedies that were woven throughout much of her life, was able to pick herself up, dust herself off, and keep on going. She was involved in the alter guild at St. Paul's and was always working at something, whether as a docent at the Virginia Museum of Art, the former home of Jefferson Davis, or the Robert E. Lee boyhood home, Minnie was always active.

Minnie and Joe lived a comfortable life in one of the large and stately homes on Monument Avenue in the Fan District of Richmond. The home had been in Minnie's family for about a hundred years and likely would have been passed on to their one son, had he not died at such an early age.

At age 62, Joe suffered a debilitating stroke and, as a result, Minnie determined that they would do better to live in a smaller home, which they purchased on River Road out near the Country Club of Virginia. Minnie secured live-in help to care for Joe until his death in 1968, at which time she decided that she could manage most of her daily affairs for herself. She secured the help of a middle-aged African American woman by the name of Annie to assist with the general upkeep of her home.

Unlike many of the women of her age, Minnie was rather open-minded, and some probably even described her as being liberal. She was well-read and didn't hesitate to speak her mind. Minnie remained engaged in life and continued to do her volunteer work. In fact it was as she was driving to the museum for her

A Granddame

afternoon volunteer effort that Minnie's car was T-boned (where one vehicle hits another vehicle in the side) by a young teenage boy headed to work at Ukrops Grocery store on Carey Street. Minnie, a very slow and methodical driver as she was in her ninth decade, had been distracted and thinking about something else and pulled into his path from a side street.

As was fitting of someone having grown up as one of the FFFVs (First Fine Families of Virginia), Minnie was always dressed to the nines. This included stockings, hat and gloves. It didn't matter that the world had changed and dress had become more casual; Minnie believed that a lady was always dressed to go out in public. And so Minnie was dressed fully.

When I encountered Minnie she had been brought into the Emergency Department at the Medical College of Virginia Hospitals, a level I trauma center, by an Henrico Ambulance Squad. They had not called a trauma team alert for her as she was awake and lucidly talking at the scene and seemed, from all indications, to be relatively stable albeit in a great deal of pain from a broken left leg and obvious broken ribs on her left side. Minnie was more concerned about looking proper as she was brought into the Emergency Department than she was necessarily worried about what might or might not happen to her.

I was busy making my rounds through the trauma emergency room when I spotted Minnie strapped to a backboard, being rolled into the ED. It quickly was determined to go ahead and place Minnie in trauma bed 2 if for no other reason than she was 83 years old and had taken quite a hit.

I took Minnie's hand, introduced myself to her; she glanced at me and smiled. It was not a smile of great discomfort but more a smile of peacefulness, almost a knowing smile. A smile that said, it's okay, I know I'm going to die. She asked me to call her nephew and her dear friend Annie. I did, and then I returned to hold her hand and soothe her furrowed brow now frozen in time.

Shortly thereafter, with now torn and tattered stockings and a skewed pink hat thrown off to the side, Minnie, who had been conversant upon arrival, had decompensated quickly and was placed

Through the Eyes of the Heart

on oxygen, repeatedly having told the doctor that she did not wish to be intubated and placed on a ventilator. Shortly thereafter, Minnie's heart stopped and because of the already broken ribs, it was determined that Minnie should be allowed to die in peace.

As I sat holding her hand, I thought about my grandmother and wondered if in fact her death had been as peaceful as Minnie's. They had both been born in 1910 and had lived in a culture that except for some technology had basically remained unchanged, at least in the eyes of the Old South. I held Minnie's hand until the monitor flat-lined and I marveled at the many places that life can and does lead us.

A life well lived! Perhaps a life ended at just the right time? Gloves, purse, and hat were placed with her effects as her body was wheeled off to the morgue. A tear of gratitude for a life that had been.

Chapter 12

A Live Oak Tree

Spring was in full bloom. There was excitement in the air, palpable on the wings of thousands of birds returning from their journeying to warmer climes for the passing winter. Excitement stirred in the heart of a young man turning a year older. Jeremy had now reached what some might call the pinnacle of adolescence and others might call the nightmare of every parent's waking moments. Jeremy turned 16, full of the promise of spring and the beginning of new adventures born in the bosom of a brand new, fire-engine red Camaro.

There had been much debate between Jeremy's parents over whether or not he should have a car as a new young driver just having received his license. Tim believed he should, and Marla was dead set against his getting a car. One of the reasons it meant so much to Tim was that he and Marla had divorced several years before, and Tim believed that this was a means of cementing his relationship with his son.

Marla's present husband Gary, Jeremy's stepfather, also believed that Jeremy should have the car. He believed it would relieve much of the burden for transport if Jeremy were driving, freeing time to be used in other ways.

So on Jeremy's 16th birthday he was presented the keys to his new ride. Jeremy was a bright young man and an excellent student, despite much of the turmoil in the lives of his parents. He was a handsome kid, still willowy and growing into his body . . . tall, six-foot-four, weighing in at 190 pounds. His blond hair, intensely blue eyes, and dimpled chin, obviously gifts received from his father. From pictures shown me by his parents, Jeremy had an amazing smile which could light up a room with the intensity of a spotlight, accompanied by wit and charm, also gifts received from his father.

Jeremy was well-loved at school and was captain of both the soccer team and the varsity basketball team and had devoted followers among the student body. As a junior, he had been nominated for Homecoming king and no doubt would have won, had he been a senior, but since he still had one more year the award was passed along to a graduating senior.

While Jeremy was extremely good-looking and precocious, he still loved nothing more than to go to the beach and run his toes through the sand as he headed toward the water, surfboard in tow. In abundant ways, Jeremy seemed older than his years would indicate, frequently drawing attention to the fact that for him quality of life was of paramount importance.

Because of his highly developed abilities, Jeremy was able to master almost anything that required physical athleticism, including surfing, windsurfing, and water skiing. In short, Jeremy was an amazing young man!

Upon completion of high school, Jeremy hoped to attend college; which one was yet to be determined. I'm sure letters of offer likely would have been coming his way. Upon completion of college he wanted to attend medical school with a plan to help others. Jeremy possessed both the intellect and the drive to take him there.

Jeremy had moved in with his dad when he was 12, preferring not to live with his mother and her new husband. Dad lived in a small house about two blocks from the boardwalk at Virginia Beach, and Mom lived about thirty miles away in a suburb of Newport News, Virginia.

A Live Oak Tree

While there was no overt rancor that existed between the divorced couple, there were definitely strains when Gary, the stepfather, attempted to put in his two cents' worth about how Tim should be parenting Jeremy. But even in the midst of that, it was clear that both parents absolutely adored Jeremy and found him to be witty, captivating, and utterly enchanting.

Of course, as is the case with many precocious children of "broken homes," Jeremy learned how to play his parents like violins to get what he wanted. He was, after all, no dolt!

Two months left of school and Jeremy would be able to spend most of the summer on the beach surfing . . .

The best roads for driving to school were, of course, the major thoroughfares; however, Jeremy much preferred the peacefulness of the back roads where he could speed without being observed and enjoy the playfulness of exploration as he fine-tuned his ability to maneuver his new vehicle through tight curves.

On this particular day, Jeremy probably was driving too fast; he missed a curve, tried to overcorrect, and went sliding on loose gravel, plowing head-on into a huge old live oak tree. Being free from many of the fetters of adolescence also somehow translated into not wearing a seatbelt. Jeremy was catapulted from his red Camaro and landed in the underbrush growing beside the road. The irony of being found lodged near death, beneath a live oak.

Who knows how much time elapsed between the impact of the crash and his being found . . . no one was quite sure. When located, he was rushed by ambulance to the nearest hospital, where doctors quickly determined that because of a closed-head injury Jeremy would best be flown to Richmond to the Medical College of Virginia Hospitals . Upon his arrival, having been stabilized previously, he immediately was admitted directly to the Neuroscience Intensive Care Unit (NSICU), a fourteen-bed unit dealing primarily with brain and spinal cord injuries.

Because Jeremy was classified as a grade III head injury, as the chaplain who provided primary coverage for that unit, I was paged to be apprised of his arrival and to let me know that family was en route.

Through the Eyes of the Heart

Head injuries are classified using a Glasgow Coma Scale (GCS); the lower the number the less likelihood of any meaningful recovery, and based on patients' placement upon that scale, they are then classified as to the level of the brain injury. Grade 1s are usually "walkie, talkies" who have a very mild concussion and are sporting a headache; grade 2s are usually fairly goofy, loud, abusive, and yet with time will recover completely; and grade 3s usually have sustained severe brain injuries and, dependent upon many factors, may or may not ever recover or live long enough to recover because of swelling to the brain. For grade 4s there is no hope for any meaningful recovery or survival. Kids, however, can and usually do defy all odds and prove you wrong at every possible turn!

With traumatic brain injuries there is always a high degree of variability. So much is dependent upon the level of down time prior to the arrival of medical intervention. Because the brain is the site of all that makes us who we are, when healthy brain function is interrupted by a lack of oxygen one can only speculate on the kind of meaningful recovery that might or might not occur.

To try to decrease the level of swelling to the brain, Jeremy was placed in a special bed that minimized the amount of stimulation that had to be given him in order to provide for ordinary activities of daily living, such as bathing, feeding, toileting, etc. Jeremy also had sustained a broken arm, collar bone, and tibia fracture along with a shattered ankle. Because of his age, Jeremy should have been placed in the Pediatric ICU, but because of his size and the nature of his injury the physicians decided that he would be best served by placing him in the NSICU.

I have never been comfortable working with pediatric patients and do so very reluctantly because of how closely they touch my heart, having lost an early adolescent myself, a decade or so prior to being involved with Jeremy, but because Jeremy was being treated in my unit I didn't believe I had much choice.

Jeremy's Glasgow Coma Scale was only a four–a pretty dismal prognosis under ordinary circumstances– but, as I said, his age left many factors unclear and up in the air. The reality was

A Live Oak Tree

clear that Jeremy was SAS or "sick as shit." His GCS indicated that he was in a deep, deep, coma–so much so that he was not able to breathe on his own, so he was placed on a ventilator with an endotracheal tube inserted in his mouth going down into his lungs and a nasogastric tube going down into his stomach to manage his stomach's secretions.

In addition to these two major mechanical supports, there were a number of other lines coming into and going out of Jeremy's body, which made one think of grapevines whose tendrils wrap around fences in early spring, each necessary for monitoring some aspect of Jeremy's bodily functions. As I looked at Jeremy's face, I could begin to see signs of blossoming raccoon eyes as the bruising from having hit his head began to emerge.

Carol, one of my favorite nurses, was working with Jeremy and trying to stabilize all of his vital signs by careful monitoring and adjusting, within the physician's specified parameters, his prescribed medications. Carol is Chinese by birth and is only about five-feet-two-inches tall. She has an infectious smile and warmth about her borne of years of doing this work and a sense of compassion that exudes from her very presence. She is always great with families, and she and I had developed quite a working relationship. On Tuesday evenings, together we facilitated a brain injury support group for families who had loved ones in the NSICU to allow them the opportunity to ask many of their unanswered questions apart from the bedside.

As Carol was briefing me on everything she knew to date about Jeremy's family, the doorbell to the unit rang, announcing the arrival of someone not yet privy to the door code. The clerk answered the door and came to tell me that there was family for Jeremy outside waiting. I left Carol, who indicated she wasn't quite yet ready for family at Jeremy's bedside and asked if I could give her another half an hour to complete her assessment and finish cleaning up Jeremy, who was still a bloody mess.

At the door I met two frantic parents! I introduced myself to them and told them that I worked with the NSICU team and would be journeying through this experience with them. I quickly took over one of the conference rooms located across the hall from the unit, and I moved them in and began hearing their and Jeremy's story. Initially present were Tim and Marla, Jeremy's parents. Others who later arrived were Jeremy's stepfather Gary, grandparents, a girlfriend of Jeremy's, and some classmates to whom he was particularly close.

As they gathered, I was doing some initial listening to them to try to figure out what they previously had been told about Jeremy's condition and to find out if they had received the opportunity to see Jeremy prior to his transfer to MCV.

What I gathered from my discussion with them was that they had been told very little other than the fact that Jeremy was in a coma, having been thrown from his car when he missed a curve and hit a huge tree head-on.

I found out that they had not been given the opportunity to see Jeremy prior to his transfer, which understandably heightened their anxiety. I also began explaining that the NSICU was a special unit, that Carol was the nurse who was caring for Jeremy, and that she was cleaning him up and getting him settled into the bed and unit. I began doing some impact previewing with them regarding what they would be seeing, hearing, and smelling as they went in to see Jeremy. One of the most difficult aspects was attempting to help them understand that Jeremy would not be able to respond to them at all, but that they should continue to reassure him of their presence and love.

One of the treatment protocols used as a part of minimizing any brain or body activity that might increase the brain swelling for patients was that through the use of medications they were paralyzed and sedated. Frequently their body temperature also was dropped by placing them on an ice blanket, again in an attempt to slow down all bodily functions which might elevate brain swelling that was already present.

On occasion, some patients might initially present with less severe brain injuries, but over the first twenty-four to forty-eight hours a patient's condition can decline quickly as the brain swelling increases.

A Live Oak Tree

In about a half an hour or so, Carol came to the conference room to meet Jeremy's parents and to prep them additionally for seeing Jeremy for the first time. Then together we led them into the unit, they as if in search of the star in the East, drawn toward the corner room where Jeremy lay. I stood alongside Marla and checked my lab coat pocket to make certain I had an ammonia capsule just in case she or any of the others should become faint.

Carol asked them to keep their voices low and would not allow them even to touch Jeremy's body because his intra-cranial pressure was already dangerously high, and she didn't want to do anything that might incidentally drive it up. Because the brain is housed in a sealed cavity the skull, as the brain swells, the pressure inside the brain rises, and the only avenue open is for the brain to push down through the opening at the base of the skull through which all the cranial nerves pass, destroying the blood flow to the brainstem, which leads to brain death.

I pulled two chairs up to the bedside and encouraged Jeremy's parents to be seated. I asked if we could share a prayer together, after which Carol suggested that they may wish to be together in the family conference room as other family members and friends arrived so that they could brief them about what was going on with Jeremy. She assured them that either she or I would come and get them should there be any changes in Jeremy's status or condition.

I escorted them back to the conference room, where they were barraged with questions by others who had arrived, wanting to know and presumably understand what was going on with Jeremy. I, along with Tim and Marla, echoed what Carol had told them, with their permission. I tried to begin laying the framework of understanding for how the next few days, possibly even weeks, might go. As I talked, it was as if I was speaking with zombies caught in no man's land, speaking with overwhelmed folks who appeared dazed and dreamlike.

If you've not had the experience of working around traumatic brain injuries and hanging around the NSICU, it is a pretty difficult place to imagine or comprehend. For most people it is fairly traumatic to see the condition of patients in this unit, let alone to hear the sounds of mechanical supports. Because many traumatic brain injured patients have little to no external damage, it is difficult for most people to make sense out of something so nonsensical.

Drs. W. and B. paged me to find out where the family was. I told them where we were, and they came across to the conference room where I introduced them to those of the family I'd already met, which was only the beginning of what felt like a cast of thousands to come.

Over the next few days the hordes of visitors began to dwindle, and the isolation and initial shock began to wane and become a part of the new normal. Jeremy had his peaks and valleys and began to make slow progress, encouraging Marla and Tim to believe that their beloved child might emerge from this hellish nightmare to live his life with all of the rights and emollients thereto, far removed from hospitals and the remembrance of more challenging times.

Tim and Marla and occasionally Marla's husband Gary and a grandparent or two would show up for the NSICU family support group meeting that Carol and I resourced on Tuesday evenings. One week ran into two weeks. Jeremy continued to have intracranial pressure problems, so they took him to the operating room and removed a bone flap from his cranium. Jeremy's parents learned from the neurosurgeons that the flap could be frozen and eventually replaced as Jeremy improved. Removing the bone flap created another open space into which the brain could swell rather than having no alternative but to press against the brainstem, causing herniation—a deadly event.

As I arrived at the hospital one morning in week three I was paged by Dr. B and Dr. W, wanting to talk with Jeremy's family. Apparently Jeremy's swelling had grown progressively worse during the night, and a CT confirmed that he had, in fact, stroked out the entire left hemisphere of his brain. As Jeremy's parents met with the two doctors, the question that loomed heavily in the air was, "Is he likely to die?"

The answer was always one of uncertainties; while he might live, a picture of how he might live began to emerge—a living death,

A Live Oak Tree

a vital, beautiful young man confined to a wheelchair, unlikely to be able to speak or understand language! Those parts of his brain were gone in the twinkling of an eye, as quickly as a blackboard can be erased.

Sad, heartsick eyes, once filled with hopefulness for what might have been, now dulled by the reality of what likely would be. Faces which seemed to be rutted by the tears and strain of the last few weeks coalesced into a sea of faces stunned by the reality of what previously they'd only feared; not wanting to believe, but somehow knowing that life would never again be the same for Jeremy... or them.

Jeremy, their young, vital surfer with a zest for life–this couldn't be! But it was. Could they do what their beloved son many times had instructed them to do? Tim was ready to honor Jeremy's wishes to remove the mechanical supports and be allowed to die peacefully; Marla and Gary were bargaining for more time, hoping that perhaps in a few more days Jeremy's prognosis might look... different. The sands of time continued to fall one grain at a time.

Several days passed and with heavy hearts, the decision was made to let go of the delusion of a different outcome. Medication maintaining Jeremy in a paralyzed and sedated condition had been stopped several days before, and Jeremy's body had exhibited no signs of any life still present within his young body although he had pupils which sluggishly responded to light. He had no other signs that there was any meaningful life left within his young, vulnerable body–a young life gone strangely out of kilter.

Decisions finally were made to remove him from all mechanical supports and to let him die the peaceful death he had already begun several weeks prior to intervention. Jeremy's body finally found peace and rest, while his bereft parents could only find sadness and grief.

I rarely attended funeral services for patients in an attempt to protect myself from the emotional vulnerability. I attended Jeremy's... maybe as my way of honoring and touching that place of resident grief found within myself! I don't know. What I do know is that my life was forever changed because of this 16-year-old's too-brief life. I know that I'm a more grateful human being and will always remember the pain in Tim and Marla's faces along with the sense of relief that Jeremy would never have to exist in a way that he would have abhorred.

Chapter 13

A New Roof

Edward turned 65 on May 19th. A memorable day for many reasons, the least of which was that two days before while repairing a few shingles on their roof, Ed fell off, shattering his spine and recreating him as a vent-dependent C_1-C_2 quadriplegic.

For those of you who may not know, there are seven cervical spine vertebrae. The lower the number, the higher up the spinal column the fracture is. Because the cranial nerves, along with motor nerves (the ones that control all movement), run through the spinal column, when the nerves are severed all movement below the fracture ceases. At a lower level, say C_4 or below, an individual still might be able to breathe on his or her own while he or she may have limited or only gross motor movement.

In Edward's case, other than speech and eye movement, he was rendered incapable of any other physical movement. What that meant for his life was that he was completely dependent upon others for every aspect of his activities of daily living, including breathing, eating, and elimination.

When I first met Edward it was a couple of days after his accident. Because of the likelihood of swelling obscuring any potential movement, the physicians were unprepared to offer any reasonable prognosis until the swelling from the injury to his neck had an opportunity to resolve and assessments could be made.

From the outset, Edward made it very clear that he had a living will and that he didn't want to continue living as a quadriplegic. Of course, one of the most challenging aspects of that was that because Edward had been stabilized at the scene and been placed on a ventilator, he was not at risk for immediate or imminent death, therefore rendering the living will virtually useless.

The courts passed the Patient Self-Determination Act in 1990. While it addressed some scenarios, it neglected to speak to a variety of issues which fall into the gray areas of ethical decision-making. Edward's was one of those cases.

Over the next several weeks, Edward remained resolute that he did not wish to continue living as a quadriplegic. It was at this point that the physicians determined that any improvements which might have occurred for Edward already had happened. Because Edward was of sound mind and infirm body, it was decided that the courts needed to be involved to establish his level of competency to make decisions.

Edward's family was very involved in his care and took turns rotating in and out of the unit so that Edward would never be without one of his family in attendance. In addition to his wife Beth, Edward had three daughters and one son, all of whom were married. Unlike Edward, who never wavered in his determination to die, his children, more so than his wife, often waffled between not wanting to let go of their dad and their awareness that he had every right to make the decision to terminate the use of mechanical supports, which would result in his death.

Once a judge determined Edward's competency, then the question arose about his mental state to make such a radical decision to terminate his life since he obviously was dealing with issues of situational depression. So in order to make certain that Edward's decision to die was not being affected by his depression, he was placed on an antidepressant, which then meant waiting an additional three weeks for the medication to cross the blood/brain

A New Roof

barrier and for him to have a full therapeutic dose of an antidepressant on-board.

Beth, while not wanting to "lose" her husband, felt as though that already had occurred when Edward fell off the roof, and because of that she became more and more aloof and seemingly disengaged. I felt relatively certain that she was trying to protect herself and was already engaging in some anticipatory grief work. The children kept up their routines of constant vigilance and never seemed to falter in their desire to hang on to their dad.

One Thursday afternoon, Kathy, Edward's primary nurse, the neurosurgeons, and I decided we needed to have a family conference at Edward's bedside to make some determinations about either moving Edward to a long-term care facility that could handle ventilator-dependent patients or honor his request to terminate his life.

While Beth and I had become relatively close and had many conversations in which she shed her tears of soul-shaking sadness, their children seemed to view me as the angel of death and really kept me at arm's length. Because of their reticence to discuss anything other than Edward's complete recovery, I thought it best that I not be in attendance at the family conference; highly unusual for me, but exceptionally important in this case!

As reported to me, during the family conference Edward, who had been unwavering in his decisions to die peacefully, remained steadfast. It was determined that on Friday the whole family would spend the night together in his room and then on Saturday morning at 9 O'clock, Edward would be given some sedation and taken off the ventilator and allowed to die peacefully.

On Saturday morning I was in attendance, not so much to support Edward's family as to make certain that the staff who had to carry out Edward's wishes were cared for during a very difficult and sad time. Edward and his family had become a regular part of the Neuroscience Intensive Care Unit for more than three months and had formed significant bonds with many of the staff members.

As 9 a.m. approached, I could sense a real change in the level of unease that Edward's children previously had expressed toward me. They even invited me to join them for prayer prior to disconnecting Edward from the ventilator, and together we sang hymns from their primitive Baptist tradition, ushering Edward into his much longed-for death and release from a life in which he no longer wished to be a part. At my encouragement, as we waited for Edward's heart to stop, which took about ten minutes from the time the ventilator was disconnected, his family shared many words of farewell and love as Edward transitioned into death.

The law and the health-care delivery system had created a complicated and convoluted scenario around Edward's death. Yet the outcome was exactly the same; maybe not exactly the same because his family did get to be present with him in his final days and had the opportunity to work through some of their uncertainty related to his death.

Maybe one day we'll get it right and recognize that we are finite creatures living in a finite world.

Chapter 14

After Hours

Donald was a really challenging kid growing up! By the time he entered middle school he had begun using alcohol and drugs and quickly discovered that his life was better, or at least that he felt "better," more confident and less likely to appear as a nerd when he was actively using. Preacher's kids (PKs) frequently are labeled as being somewhat nerdy anyway, and Donald was no exception. Donald Jr. was an only child born to Donald and Marge when Donald was almost 40 and Marge was 37.

Donald Jr's. father was an Episcopal priest serving as an assistant rector at an often-considered elite church. It was thought by many to be elite because a large number of those in attendance were affluent and influential in the community. Early on in his career Donald had decided to remain an assistant rector so that he could devote as much time as possible to his family and for the satisfaction of working with the homeless of the community.

His wife Marge taught in the Richmond school district. She had helped many a young person find and extricate him or herself from the self-perpetuating circumstances of generational poverty that loomed large among the African American population in downtown Richmond City Schools. Together Donald and Marge had done a tremendous amount within the community and had become well-respected and widely known for being people of real substance and quality. In my role at the Medical College of Virginia Hospitals I had the occasion to meet Donald once when he came to visit a parishioner who had been injured in an automobile crash. I liked him immensely, and we forged a bond almost instantly.

As chaplain and coordinator of bereavement services, I made it a point not to read the newspapers or watch the local news; it was my way of emotionally detaching from the daily work that I did. So you can understand my surprise when I was walking down the hall, heading to my office on a Monday morning when I encountered Donald, who introduced me to his wife. Both appeared weary and somewhat disheveled. They and other members of their family were camped all over the ICU waiting room, which was right next door to my office.

I stopped to ask them what was going on as I'd not heretofore seen them in the ICU waiting room. They told me that their son had been shot and was in the Neuroscience Intensive Care Unit (NSICU). I explained to them that I was the chaplain who worked with that particular unit. I have to admit that my own stereotypes were running wild because they did not look like most of the families of victims with gunshot wounds with whom I came in contact. I excused myself for a couple of minutes and went to my office to deposit my belongings, grabbed my lab coat, and then went to the unit to find out what this was all about.

When I arrived in the NSICU and located Donald's bed, it didn't take but a couple of minutes for me to figure out that "this" was not likely to go well. I found out what I could from Jim, the nurse caring for him, and the chart and went back to visit with Donald's parents.

Donald Sr. was sitting alone in the waiting room when I returned; Marge had gone for some breakfast. Donald proceeded to tell me that because of his role at the church, he was not accustomed to being in the position of asking for help; he was traditionally the one offering it! I assured him that I understood some of the challenges and discomfort that brought as I'm quite sure if

After Hours

the situation were reversed I too would have been feeling similarly awkward and uncomfortable.

I asked Donald if he could fill me in on what had happened as he understood it. I had received some information from the duty chaplain in morning report, but because of the volume of cases discussed each morning I can't say that I really tuned in or immediately made the connections with this particular event. Generally I preferred to visit with families and glean my information from them about what they believed happened as well as to ascertain their knowledge about their loved one's condition and prognosis.

What Donald Sr. told me was that Donald Jr. in early adolescence had begun using alcohol and drugs as a means of coping with his social anxiety. He used for a number of years and was arrested by the law for breaking and entering in order to support his habit. After having spent time in juvenile detention, Donald had pulled his life together, and because he was under 18 at the time, his record had been expunged. And now, several years later, he had entered into a management track with "Fred's Ice Cream Shop," a nationally known chain in which he had progressed rapidly and became the evening manager for this particular store located in Richmond's Northside.

As evening manager on duty, when closing the store for the night, the practice was that once the store was empty of patrons the doors were locked and then the evening manager would move the money from the cash register into the safe until it could be taken to the bank the following day. This particular night the perpetrator must have been hiding in the bathroom until after the exterior doors were locked and then made his or her presence known. Only two employees were left in the store at the time, Donald Jr., the manager on duty, and an assistant manager.

At gunpoint, the two managers were placed on the floor, side by side, face down. The keys to the register were taken and then the perpetrator shot both of the managers. The assistant manager died immediately, but Donald Jr. had been rushed to the Medical College of Virginia, having been shot in the head. I listened with horror as Donald told me the story, and my heart wept for the death I anticipated would be coming their way. What a sad way to die after all Donald Jr. had been through to restore his life to a place of respectability.

I know I have a deep, abiding trust in God, but I have to admit that there are times when I sure question: Why . . . ?

Because of the location of Donald Jr.'s brain injury, it was possible that he might survive, but as what? Fortunately, they would never need to worry about that possibility as Donald Jr.'s brain swelling would finish what the gunman's bullet had begun, but it would take several days. What a travesty!

After a few days, Donald and Marge looked like shadows of themselves, apparitions haunted by the possibilities of what might yet lay before them . . .

Donald and Marge attended the NSICU family group that Carol and I facilitated on Tuesday evenings. They were supportive of other parents who had family members in the unit, and Donald in particular had a tough time stepping out of his role as caregiver. Donald and Marge both gave lip service to the fact that whatever happened, they knew they would be okay. I believe that they had both begun to recognize that the likelihood of a "good" outcome was slim to none for Donald Jr.

On Wednesday Donald, Sr. and I talked, and he shared with me that Donald Jr. had been a very gifted pianist and that he and Marge already had decided that should Donald die, any memorial gifts in honor of Donald Jr. would be used to place pianos on each unit at Westminster Canterbury, a Presbyterian/Episcopalian retirement facility located in Richmond, Virginia.

That afternoon Donald Jr.'s intracranial pressure shot sky high, forcing his brain to push down upon his brainstem, causing herniation. Donald Jr.'s driver's license had him listed as being an organ donor, and both of his parents already had made certain that if he should be able to be an organ donor that he would have wanted that; therefore, they wanted to fulfill his wishes, if at all possible.

When I heard their wish expressed, I contacted LifeNet, the organ procurement agency in that area of Virginia. Their representative arrived within the hour, and after looking at lab values and at Donald Jr.'s body it was decided that because of his previous use of illegal drugs he was too high a risk for HIV, and so he was ineligible to be an organ donor.

Donald and Marge were both devastated. They had held out the hope that in this craziness perhaps Donald Jr.'s life could take on some sense of meaning by helping others; when they heard the crushing news they both "crashed" and came tumbling apart. After about a half hour of gut-wrenching tears, they pulled themselves together and announced that they were ready to go home. I walked them to their car with empty hands and emptier hearts now stained with tears forever.

A couple of years later while visiting a friend and resident at Westminster/Canterbury, I saw a piano in one of the many dayrooms. I looked at the plaque mounted on it and sure enough, it was in memory of Donald Jr.

May the music of life continue to ring in your long-silenced heart!

Chapter 15

Business as Usual

One Saturday morning in late May my pager went off with a call-back number that I knew only too well! I'm guessing it was probably about 9 a.m., and I was out by the pool cleaning trash out of the flow valves, getting ready to take a dip. While it was very atypical for me to get a call on my personal pager on the weekend, I was after all on back-up call, so it wasn't like it never previously had happened.

I anticipated a quick call to reassure a "chaplain resident," then back to business as usual; however, that was not the way it was to go. When I called the Trauma ER, Link, the resident on call, must have been sitting on top of the phone waiting. He answered almost immediately.

He sounded pretty frazzled and proceeded to tell me that he'd had an awful night and had just received notice that there were four trauma room cases being brought in from a high-speed roll-over crash. Additionally, the folks from Channel 12 News were there to do a story about the kinds of experiences that were dealt with in a Trauma ER on a daily basis. The question hanging in Link's voice as if suspended from a high wire was, "Can you come in and help?"

"Sure! Let me throw some clothes on and grab my lab coat, and I'll be there shortly."

Business as Usual

When I arrived, Campbell Brown, the news reporter from Channel 12 (who later went on to be one of the anchors in New York for the weekend *Today Show* on NBC) was there waiting to talk and ask questions, and Link was waiting to head up to the Pediatric Intensive Care Unit to respond to another page he'd received recently. So I walked into the trauma room with all four beds occupied, the patients having arrived only a short while before me.

Trauma bed 1 was usually kept for the most critical, and they descended in level of severity down to bed 4, which as triaged, was almost always the least critical in a "high trauma" situation. Before Link left he informed me that no one yet had been identified, and I could tell by doing a visual scan of the room that the patient in trauma bed 1 was deceased. As I listened I realized that while she had been transported, it really had been determined she was DOS (Dead on the Spot), and treatments had been stopped immediately upon arrival in the Emergency Department.

Since all four patients had been there for a short while by the time I arrived, I began at bed 4, trying to figure out who was who and then find and contact family members. As I spoke with the patient in bed 4 and reassured him that he was doing fine (from what I had been told), I began to piece together bits of the story as to what had happened to bring them into the ED. That patient's name was Jason, and, other than some small cuts which were sutured, he had non-life-threatening injuries and was moved quickly out of the trauma room.

I learned from Jason that the four were all students at the same high school, and they had gone to graduation the night before and then on to a party to celebrate the fact that they had now left behind their status as "lowly juniors" and had achieved new status as seniors. As he talked and shared what he could remember, I began asking about the other three patients. What might he know about them? Turned out he knew the patients in beds 2 and 3 and gave me their names. He said he really didn't know who the other "chick" with dark hair was, although he thought he'd heard someone at the party call her Amanda, but he had no clue about her last name.

Knowing that there were parents out there whose daughter had died in trauma bed 1, I knew I needed to make every effort to find out who the young woman was! First, I called the state police and found out that the officer working the scene was Officer Flenner. I was told that he would be on his way to the ER as soon as he had completed the paperwork at the scene and could get free. I asked the dispatcher if he had any contact info, which he did not, and I gave him the names of the three that I had been able to piece together from the patient in bed 4, for which he was very grateful. He had nothing on the unidentified young woman.

As I spoke with the patient in trauma bed 3, I found that her name was Rachael. I held her hand and encouraged her to slow-chest breathe with me as the orthopedic resident manipulated her broken femur. She asked me whether everyone was okay; I learned many years ago that unless someone asked me the question three times about how someone was doing when in fact that person had died, I sort of brushed aside their question and provided rather vague answers. In this instance I brushed aside Rachael's question and began to ask her if she knew who everyone was. She too didn't know Amanda's last name, as they had only recently met at school, but Rachael did tell me that her mother worked in the office at the school and in all probability knew who Amanda was. Rachel gave me her parents' phone number and I asked if it was okay for me to call them. I called and was able to get a home phone number for Amanda's mother.

After I finished speaking with Rachael's mother, I stretched the cord for the phone to what felt like halfway across the world so she could speak with Rachel; she needed the reassurance that all was okay with her daughter or at least would be with time. After a few moments of their conversation, I retrieved the phone and explained to her mother that I still was trying to find identification for Amanda and asked whether she knew what Amanda's last name might be. She said that she didn't know it but that Amanda's

Business as Usual

mom worked at the rural post office close to their home and she would be glad to go by and tell her to go to the hospital on her way. Internally I breathed a sigh of relief that I had been rescued from having to call Amanda's mother and had been assured that Rachael's mother was going by to let Amanda's mother know what had happened. Relieved—Why? I'm not quite sure I know, except that perhaps I wouldn't have to continue to carry alone the burden of the knowledge that her daughter had died!

Rachael's mom knew the parents of the others as well and was going to get in touch with them too. Recognizing that I probably had at least forty-five minutes before any of them would likely arrive at the hospital, I took a few minutes to visit with Campbell Brown, who interviewed me about my role on the Trauma team. She had watched me going from one bed to the next, holding a hand, reassuring a scared and frightened young person, and gathering what she assumed was pertinent information.

The patient in trauma bed 2 had been taken to the operating room because of internal bleeding. Rachael had been given medication to sedate her as they set and cast her femur, the long bone connecting the hip and the knee, and then she was being sent for a CAT scan before being moved out of the trauma room along with Jason. I knew then that I was only waiting on the parents of Amanda to arrive. I looked over at trauma bed 1 where Amanda's body lay lifeless and battered beyond recognition, and I wondered how I was going to care for her parents. God love them!

In the midst of the initial chaos of traumas, time seems to fly by very quickly, but now that the quiet and ordinary had replaced chaos, time began to march by at the speed of an ant trying to make its way across a football field. After about an hour and a half elapsed since I first contacted Rachael's mother and I had yet to hear anything from any family about Amanda, I began to wonder whether she in fact had been unable to reach them; but then a somewhat frantic yet cautious and even skeptical call came in to the ED from a woman who had been told that her daughter may have been brought into the ED from a car accident.

Through the Eyes of the Heart

The ER clerk quickly passed the phone call off to me. How is my daughter doing? Not knowing this person on the other end of the phone or having any way to confirm that Amanda was in fact her daughter, I was very cautious about what information I gave. Also, I hardly wanted to blurt out to someone who still had to drive to the hospital that her daughter was probably dead. She identified herself as Grace and told me that she did have a 17-year-old daughter whom she'd been told may have been brought in from a car crash.

I introduced myself on the phone and told her that I would be on the lookout for her arrival at the hospital. The question of how her daughter was doing still hung in the air as I answered that they were working on a young woman and that she probably needed to come to MCV to the emergency room. I assured her that they were doing everything they could do and that I would be watching for her. She told me that they were on their way, leaving me to wonder who the "they" were.

Because one never knows how quickly the trauma room is going to be needed again, bodies of the deceased are rarely kept in there for any great length of time. If I had known what time Amanda's parents might arrive, I would have postponed sending her body to the morgue, but since I had no idea, nor did I know if this was their daughter or how much longer it might take to them to arrive, I reluctantly agreed to let the transportation aide move the young woman's body to the morgue. In my role as chaplain and coordinator of bereavement services for the hospitals, I had that kind of authority, and the medical and nursing staff generally went along with whatever recommendations I made.

The hours ticked by. Greg, the state trooper with whom I'd spoken earlier and who was the investigating officer at the crash site, arrived at the hospital. He and I had a chance to talk through our game plan for how best to deal with Amanda's parents, presuming that they were indeed this young woman's parents. Finally, almost two hours after my initial contact with Rachael's mother, Grace and Tom the alleged parents of Amanda arrived and were ushered into the family conference room.

Business as Usual

Greg and I had worked out that we were going to see the parents together upon their arrival. When we walked into the conference room, two frightened parents initially became agitated and fearful as Greg, who was obviously a state trooper, and I with a name tag stating that I was a chaplain, walked in to the conference room.

"Where is Amanda?"

"How is she doing, and where is the doctor treating her?"

They wanted to see the doctor immediately and Tom, Amanda's father, went initially from being scared to almost violent and belligerent in a split second when we explained that we did have a young woman who had been brought in from a car crash who as of yet was unidentified.

Her father got in my face and yelled, "I want to see my daughter now!"

Greg and I were playing off one another as though we had worked together as a team, for years and we were both working to try to de-escalate the situation. Greg explained that we were unable to identify the young woman and so we couldn't oblige him in his request to see her until we knew conclusively that the young woman was in fact their daughter.

Greg asked whether Amanda had any identifying marks, such as scars or birthmarks that might help us identify her. Both of her parents were shaking their heads in disbelief, not really able to grasp or comprehend this potentially devastating news all at once; they were in what I call "trauma overload." Finally, her father, who sank into a crumpled heap on the couch with his hands covering his face and tears streaming down, spoke in a hushed whisper.

"She has a clubbed thumb on her hand." He held his thumb up and said with almost impassive resignation, "It looks just like mine."

Greg and I both mentally registered the information, and I asked whether there was anyone they wanted me to call to come and be with them–a pastor, a friend?

After getting them water and showing them how to use the phone to get an outside line, Greg and I left them together wrapped in their fears as we walked to the morgue, an almost fifteen-minute walk away through eerie tunnels under the hospital, to see if we could positively identify their daughter by her clubbed thumb. As Greg and I walked and talked, my mind was racing about how best to tell Amanda's parents about the condition of their daughter's body with its almost unrecognizable and distorted facial features.

As we walked, I flashed back to being an eighth-grader when one of my high school idols, Rodney, and four friends were out joy riding on a Friday night on John's Island right outside of Charleston, South Carolina when they hit a tree head-on doing 120 mph. My friend Rodney was decapitated! I found myself wondering how his parents had been told about his death.

Deaths like Amanda's and Rodney's are never pretty, and there is very little way to "dress them up." If in fact this was Tom and Grace's daughter, as Greg and I suspected it was, I decided to be kind, gentle, and honest in describing the condition of her body. I'd leave the choice up to them about whether or not they wanted to view and remember their daughter as she was now or as they had known her in life. After all, they were the ones who were going to have to live with the disturbing images for the rest of their lives. I was only a passing player on their journey of grief.

As Greg and I arrived at the morgue and opened the refrigerator drawer into which Amanda's now-cold body had been placed, it occurred to me that we had neglected to ask the parents upon which hand we would likely find her clubbed thumb. Fortunately, we guessed the correct hand at the outset, so we only needed to partially unzip the body bag that now held Amanda's remains.

The thumb on the body's left hand was, indeed, clubbed . . .

Now we could end her parents' fears of the unknown and confirm the beginnings of their worst nightmares . . .

When Greg and I returned to the conference room, Grace's brother and sister-in-law had arrived. We walked into the room, and our countenances confirmed that the deceased young woman was their daughter, Amanda. The cries of anguish echoed off the walls as they held one another, rocked, and cried what surely must have been a river of tears. I sat with my arms encircling them both

Business as Usual

as they grieved for Amanda—and as I grieved for my friend Rodney. Together we held each other's hearts.

Amanda's aunt and uncle stood together in the corner, holding one another, and Greg stood by the door and talked quietly with them as they asked questions about what had happened. In my own head I remember questioning, does it really matter?

She was already dead, and at the same time I knew that for Grace and Tom the nightmare was only just beginning, and each of these small details would be a part of their collective grief and eventual healing. As their tears ebbed and the reality of Amanda's death began to rest heavily upon their hearts, we talked about next steps, and they shared stories about their journey together as a family.

It turned out that Grace was the postmaster for a small rural post office and part of the delay in their getting to the hospital had been waiting for the post office to close at noon so she could lock up and leave. She knew that Amanda had spent the night with a friend after having gone to this celebrative party for the juniors, so she figured there was nothing too seriously wrong with Amanda or the other parents would have called.

Amanda was an only child. Her parents had tried for about ten years to conceive and finally, when they were both almost 40, Grace wound up unexpectedly pregnant. Amanda had been their pride and joy, having been both musically and academically gifted.

As the story unfolded, it turned out too that Tom was the football coach and history teacher for the rural high school that Amanda attended. Tom had been raised by an alcoholic father and struggled his entire life with issues of low self-esteem and perfectionism. It wasn't that he expected perfection of Amanda as much as he believed he needed to be the "perfect" father and the "perfect" husband and could never quite do or be good enough to achieve his father's approval: the one for whose approval he yearned.

He and Grace had met at the post office when he moved to the community almost thirty years before. They had become best friends and eventually married, knowing that they really wanted children. As Amanda had grown into adolescence, Amanda and

Through the Eyes of the Heart

Grace had become best friends, sharing many secrets and "girl time" together. Amanda had been such a rich gift, and now she was gone!

Campbell Brown was still waiting to talk further with me when Amanda's parents finally left–with empty hands and empty hearts! How do you even begin to explain to someone what you do when it is so intimate and soul-touching? I don't remember what I said to her, but I know I said to myself that I felt so damned thankful that my son was safely at home.

At least for the moment I could leave and return to the peacefulness of the afternoon sun as it reflected on the stillness of the pool water at home, its fingers splayed out in a rainbow of hope, the spectrum reflecting the promise of a new tomorrow. The following year, I was struck again by grief as I heard that my "foxhole buddy" and new friend Officer Greg Flenner had been hit and killed by a drunk driver at a traffic stop. Business as usual, I wonder?

Chapter 16

Engaged

Rob and Jennifer were young and in love. They had known each other in high school, but it wasn't until several years later that a friend of theirs had fixed them up and they had actually begun dating. Rob was 26 and Jennifer 25. They had gone to Florida for a vacation in the late fall, which was where they became engaged.

Rob had done a very traditional proposal by getting down on one knee and proposing to Jennifer on the beach under a full moon where he presented her with a diamond ring. Jennifer initially had been very reluctant to wed because her mom was all alone since her husband, Jennifer's father, died in a fatal car crash in Vietnam when Jennifer was only 5.

In order to make her mother more comfortable with their marriage, Rob, who was particularly understanding and unselfish, determined that they should purchase a duplex with one apartment on the ground floor and the other above it on the second so that Jennifer's mother could live in close proximity and they would be able to continue to support her emotionally as she aged.

As Rob and Jennifer left their hotel to return home to Connecticut, they both expressed a desire to remain in the beauty of the location where they'd spent an enchanted week together. But alas, the real world beckoned them to return to their jobs and the ordinariness of life. As they began their journey homeward, they blended and flowed with the rest of the traffic north up the I-95 corridor.

If you've ever traveled I-95, you know what a crazy, busy stretch of road it becomes as you enter Virginia, heading north toward all of the major cities up the Eastern seaboard. Because it is almost a twenty-hour trip from Florida to Connecticut, Rob and Jennifer had already made arrangements to spend the night in Washington to break up the trip and to do some sightseeing prior to returning home.

As the weather can be during the fall of the year, it was fairly blustery, interspersed with thunderstorms, causing the visibility to be reduced greatly and the traffic to be flowing at a somewhat slower pace than usual, punctuated by the occasional "hot rodder" trying to make good time. As twilight approached and the air temperature began to drop, a heavy fog enveloped them, lowering the visibility to about ten feet in front of the car.

Rob, who had been driving for many years, knew that in order to make it to Washington they would need to push on through, so he marked the taillights of a tractor-trailer in front of them and kept up as best as he could. By late afternoon it had been a wearing day as the traffic had been particularly heavy, but they were still moving along and slowly began their journey past Richmond where the afternoon "traffic rush" usually begins around 3:30.

About ten miles north of Richmond the traffic was still running heavily and the visibility was poor as dusk descended and a tractor-trailer began to edge over into the right hand lane where Rob and Jennifer were traveling. As the truck eased over into their lane, Rob sat on the horn, but the truck kept coming, forcing them onto the shoulder where they hit a pothole that sent them careening off the edge of the shoulder. The vehicle flipped over and over and over again. While Rob had been seat belted and remained in the vehicle trapped, Jennifer had been unbelted and was jettisoned from the car before the second revolution of the vehicle occurred.

Rob remained trapped as nighttime descended into blackness, not sure where he was or what had happened. Retrospectively

Engaged

he told me he thought he might have briefly lost consciousness but really couldn't remember anything about what had happened or why he was where he was, trapped in his seatbelt with a caved-in roof compressing against his head. Initially he could see shadows moving around him as the setting sun peeked through the fog and splayed its fingers of light across the ravine where he found himself.

As Rob began to gain some sense of awareness and the clouds of disorientation began to lift, he became aware that his left arm was killing him. He also became aware of hanging upside down, suspended from his seatbelt. He could hear voices close by but seemed to be in a void floating in and out of altered consciousness.

When they were forced off the shoulder they went into a ravine, Jennifer went airborne, landing probably 25 yards from the place the car finally came to rest. Gratefully she was not alert or aware enough to recognize the nature of injuries she had sustained. She actually looked relatively peaceful, albeit out of place lying quietly and serenely at the bottom of the ravine, as reported to me by the rescue squad.

The state police had called for Medflight, and they carefully loosened Rob from the seatbelt to the sound of his screams as they moved his battered body. They located Jennifer because Rob kept calling for a woman even though they were unsure of where or who she was.

MCV Hospitals in downtown Richmond, Virginia was the closest level I trauma center, so Jennifer was flown there, being the most critically injured. Rob was transported by Hanover County Ambulance Service, arriving about twenty minutes after Jennifer. Upon arrival in the trauma room it was determined relatively quickly that there was nothing that could be done for Jennifer, and she was declared with a time of death of 6:32 p.m.

One of the lessons I learned through years of trauma room work as a chaplain was if people asked about a loved one three times then they were actually ready to hear whatever it was I needed to tell them. When Rob rolled into the trauma room in excruciating pain, he was not nearly as seriously injured, so he was placed in trauma bed 3 and he asked where Jennifer was (first time). I shared with him that she was in trauma bed 1 and they were working on her.

They quickly drew bloods and sent Rob to X-ray, and upon his return he once again asked me how Jennifer was doing (second time). I assured him that they were doing everything possible for her. I remained with him as the physicians and nurses continued their assessment, allowing him to squeeze two fingers on my left hand to help him through the painful moments. In between sets of physicians, Rob told me their story and shared that they were headed home to tell Jennifer's mother that they had become engaged.

It was after the orthopedic resident set Rob's arm and checked its placement that Rob asked me a (third time) how Jennifer was doing. I took a deep breath and told him that Jennifer had died. A sorrowful howl issued forth from him like a wounded animal, and the tears coursed down his cheeks in rivulets. He spoke of the injustice, screaming over and over again, "it's not fair, she didn't deserve that."

In age, I easily could have been Rob's father, and I stroked his forehead and listened as he raged and still clung to my fingers. After awhile Rob's shouts dwindled to paroxysms of soft sobbing, punctuated by periodic statements of "it's not fair," with my words echoing in his ears: "You're right, it's not fair."

After what seemed like a lifetime, my cheeks also damp with tears, I began the process of determining legal next of kin, asking Rob if he knew about family for Jennifer for the purpose of death notification. He informed me that Jennifer's father had been killed in Vietnam when she was a young child and that her mother had never remarried. He didn't know her address or phone number, but he did know her mother's name and the city in which she lived.

Jennifer had left home right after high school and moved to New York, which was where she and Rob had met. On their way home from this trip they were planning on stopping off in Connecticut so that Jeff could meet Jennifer's mother and they could begin to discuss wedding plans.

Engaged

Under ordinary circumstances, I would never share the news of a death over the phone, but given the distance, I determined that it was equally unfair to ask Jennifer's mother to drive all the way from Connecticut to Virginia to be told that her daughter was dead. So, armed with a place and a name, I contacted the special assistance operator to try to track down a phone number for Jennifer's mom. Twenty minutes later, after many hoops and much red tape, I was able to retrieve a phone number, and I dialed the number, taking a few deep breaths as the phone rang to try and calm the jitters that clung to my stomach and migrated to my shaking hands as I waited for an answer. As it rang, I found myself hoping that no one would answer. Such was not the case.

When a woman answered the phone, I introduced myself, and after confirming that she had a daughter by the name of Jennifer with the same date of birth as the deceased young woman, I explained that Jennifer had been in a car crash returning home from Florida. I proceeded to ask if she was alone. She said that she was, so I asked if she had any neighbors who were close by that she would feel comfortable asking to come over for a few minutes; she assured me that she did. I asked her to please get her neighbor and that I would like to speak to the neighbor when she returned to the phone.

I waited patiently, dreading being the one to drop the bomb into this woman's life that her only child was dead but simultaneously trusting that what I was doing was the kindest way to handle this unusual situation. Ten minutes passed and finally a woman came on the phone, and after introducing myself to her I shared with her the news that I was going to share with Jennifer's mother so that she would be in the best position to support her friend.

I then got back on the phone with Jennifer's mother and told her what had happened as kindly and tenderly as I could, all the while feeling incredibly helpless knowing that there was nothing I could do to ameliorate the pain this mother was most likely experiencing. She listened with rapt attention interspersed with sobbing as I struggled to keep my voice from cracking with emotion as I spoke with her; after I answered her questions as best as I could, again I asked to speak to the neighbor.

I provided the neighbor the name and phone number of the hospital and told her who it was she needed to contact when Jennifer's mother made decisions about funeral arrangements and the disposition of her daughter's body. I also gave her the name and phone number of a local funeral home that I was confident would be glad to work with her mother to transport Jennifer's body back to Connecticut.

After I concluded the business with the neighbor, Jennifer's mother asked again to speak to me. She thanked me for my kind call and asked if she might speak to Rob. I assured her that she could but that it would take me a minute to arrange to get him to a phone. I placed her on hold and switched to a phone in the trauma room and stretched it across to him, having given him the reassurance that I would remain with him. Together they cried with Rob saying over and over again, "I'm so sorry, I'm so sorry."

I gathered that she must have been very kind to him and after obtaining contact information for him, Jennifer's mother hung up. I then helped Rob contact some friends in New York who were going to come down and help him return home.

Home: a strange word for a place now laced with empty memories and haunts of what might have been!

Chapter 17

I-95 Southbound

I usually like to listen to the headline news in the morning while I'm getting dressed. This particular mid-September day I remember hearing the reporters talk about snarled traffic on the southbound side of the Interstate between Richmond and Petersburg, Virginia.

The truck traffic on I-95 between Washington and Petersburg is always densely packed and runs thick with semi-tractor trailers. On this particular occasion I can't remember if a truck had dumped a load in the middle of the highway or if there had been an accident, but whatever the cause of the traffic jam, the news was reporting that traffic on I-95 southbound was slowed to a crawl.

Jeff and Paula were in their RV headed from New Jersey to Florida where they planned to spend the winter. Jeff had retired earlier that year, and he and Paula had wrestled with whether or not he should retire so early, but they had some other friends who had retired and traveled back and forth to Florida in their RV, and they kept encouraging Jeff and Paula to join them in their vagabond lifestyle.

Finally Jeff and Paula decided that this was what they wanted, and fortunately they found a late-model used RV with low mileage. So, they purchased it and set off to begin their life as snowbirds.

Jeff and Paula had been married since finishing high school and were to celebrate their forty-sixth anniversary in December. Jeff had done well as an auto mechanic and liked to tinker with engines and older vehicles so for him this RV was a dream come true! It provided him the opportunity to keep work and play combined under one roof, so to speak.

Paula had been content as a homemaker, and although they never had children, she had managed to fill her time doing volunteer work and being a dedicated and supportive spouse. Her life had been defined by Jeff's.

As they traveled this particular morning, they had been discussing whether they thought they would like to continue being snowbirds every year. While they loved the landscape and beaches of Florida, they anticipated that they would really miss their lifelong friends and bowling companions in New Jersey; no decisions were made.

As they sat in the snarled traffic on I-95, Jeff began to hear a strange clicking noise coming from somewhere under the RV. Not sure whether it was mechanical or not, Jeff pulled the RV out of traffic and onto the shoulder in order to have a look see. He first checked the back of the RV to make certain that everything was well secured, and then he made his way to the front to check under the hood of the engine.

Unbeknownst to either of them, an eighteen-wheeler was barreling down the interstate, running wide open. The driver was behind schedule and attempting to make up some lost time. As he rounded the curve in the road, he could see the traffic backup ahead and began applying his brakes. He previously had received notice about needing to get his brakes repaired, but he also had to continue to earn a living, so he decided to make this run and then take a couple of days off to make the necessary repairs.

When the trucker realized that his brakes were not going to allow him to stop without careening into the vehicles stopped in front of him, he whipped his truck onto the shoulder in anticipation of buying some extra braking distance.

I-95 Southbound

Meanwhile Jeff had determined that the abnormal sound he had heard was something hung up in his right front wheel well. As he climbed under the RV to dislodge the offending branch, the eighteen-wheeler came charging down the shoulder, realizing far too late that he was going to hit the rear of the parked RV.

All the while, Paula had been turned around in her seat, watching the line of slow-moving traffic. She briefly caught a glimpse of the oncoming tractor-trailer in the driver's side view mirror right before it hit the rear of the RV. Between her own deafening screams she both viscerally heard and felt the wheels bump as they were pushed over Jeff's body from behind. What followed was a timeless blur of silence punctuated by Jeff's screams from under the wheels of the RV as it was pushed over him.

After some time, Jeff was extricated from beneath the wheels of the RV and was flown the twenty-plus miles to MCV Hospitals as the trauma team was alerted. Accordingly, I was waiting at the door as they rolled into the trauma room with Jeff still screaming in agony as he quickly crashed and died.

My friend Lanny, one of the flight paramedics, told me that Jeff's wife was on the scene, but that was as much as he knew. So I waited...

In about an hour and a half two women arrived at the ER registration looking for Jeff, and they were escorted into the family conference room, which was where I met them.

"How is Jeff doing?" The word's hung in the air like leaves tacitly dropping from the trees in early fall.

I introduced myself and responded that they were still working on Jeff in order to buy myself time to try and find one of the ER doctors to come and talk with Paula. I finally found Dr. D. to come in and tell Paula that Jeff had died shortly after his arrival. Paula crumbled in a sobbing heap on the sofa. I sat on the arm of the sofa with my hand resting gently upon her shoulder as she cried in anger, fear, frustration, and aloneness. After some lapse of time, Paula began to pull herself together and asked, "How did Jeff die?"

"I'm not sure I understand what you're asking," I said.

"Was his death peaceful, did he have anything to say before he died?"

It was then that I understood she was looking for some sense of loving closure from the man with whom she'd lived, loved, and shared the bulk of her life.

At this point I had a decision to make. Jeff's death was anything but peaceful. He had been screaming in agonal pain when he first arrived, which was quickly replaced by silence as he slipped into death. Without answering her, I asked her to tell me about Jeff.

As she began talking, a peaceful and serene expression replaced anguish on her face, displacing her look of tortured agitation and fear as she talked about Jeff's gentle and loving spirit. She told me how they'd met and a little bit about their wonderful marriage. As I listened I formulated in my mind an answer to Paula's question. And when she finished sharing her remembrances, I returned to her previous question.

"You asked me earlier about Jeff's death."

"Jeff died a very peaceful death, I was by his side," –which was true. "He asked me to tell you that he loved you."

At this point tears slipped down her cheeks, and she appeared more fragile and less capable than I initially had experienced her.

She looked up at me through her tears and gave me a feeble smile and said, "Thank you."

I offered to take her in to see his body, which she decided she wanted to do. I walked with the new widow and her friend, who had traveled in caravan with Paula and Jeff, into the trauma room, which had been cleaned up. Jeff's body had been covered with clean sheets, not in an effort to present an illusion of life and belying the reality of the death he had sustained, but to promote a less dramatic view of a gruesome and gory death.

Paula patted Jeff's hand and kissed his now-cold forehead, and we walked back into the family conference room together. Paula now turned her attention to what needed to happen next. We talked about possible funeral homes and choices, and she indicated that Jeff had always wanted to be cremated. Hearing that, I

I-95 Southbound

asked if she wanted me to contact the Cremation Society: a representative came and spoke with her about that option.

Paula chose to have Jeff's body cremated, and I made arrangements with a local hotel for her to stay in until the following day when the cremains would be cooled, ready to be picked up and transported back home to New Jersey. Her friend made the necessary arrangements to spend the night with Paula and to drive her back to New Jersey the following day.

I gave them directions to the hotel and walked them to her friend's vehicle and sent them on their way, the void palpable and profound. A happy marriage and life shared together, now shattered and lost forever!

Chapter 18

One Train Track Too Many

At 9 a.m. my trauma pager went off, alerting me that my morning routine was about to change. Closing out a conversation in which I was engaged, I quickly moved down a gray stairwell to take my place among the rest of the team as we checked in with the trauma recorder. The faces of all of us who were waiting mirrored the color of the stairwell I'd come down. It was early and we didn't normally get trauma calls until later in the day, after we'd at least been awake for a short while; definitely not a favorite way to begin a day that had every potential to be emotionally demanding, ending in acute fatigue.

As we stood together, the nurses, physicians, radiology technicians, medical students, residents, and I awaiting the arrival of the Medflight crew, we were laughing and talking about our lives apart from the Emergency Department. We were bonding in strange and unique ways sharing stories that only other "foxhole buddies" could ever begin to understand or appreciate; each of us attempting to dispel our anxieties about what was about to roll through our doors and change our day and more often than not touch our lives in significant ways too.

The pendulum swung back and forth seemingly in slow motion as the minutes of the "Golden Hour" flitted away like

One Train Track Too Many

monarch butterflies headed south for the winter. In the distance a radio squawked, sounding like a formation of geese, reporting that Medflight had landed and announcing that CPR was in progress and their estimated time of arrival was 10 minutes, the length of time it took to get from the helicopter pad to the Trauma Room. Time passed slowly as we waited.

Finally, a flurry of activity as the remnants of the pale body of a young woman were transferred from a Medflight gurney to a more sophisticated trauma bed and folks awkwardly replaced one another doing CPR: 1, 2, 3, 4, 5 breathe–the sound of an ambu bag honking as the diaphragm sucked in fresh air.

The air was immediately redolent with the smell and taste of copper as a trail of blood flowed down the hall and a pool of it encircled the gurney upon which a young woman now lay. There were shouts which became a deafening roar: "We've got to get her to the operating room NOW!"

"What's the situation with family?" I asked of no one in particular. Permission for surgery having been granted by the patient representative, another flurry of activity ensued as the team rolled toward the OR. The image that came to my mind watching them was of ants hovering over the body of a dead caterpillar, each sucking out more of the life which once was present and was now all but gone. Like a group of ants, each one of the players knew his or her part and performed it with expert precision.

"What's her name" I asked.

"Kelly–Wills, Wells, Widmarck, Wallcup . . . the parents were at the scene and should be here shortly."

As they moved Kelly to the operating room, a lull once again settled in. Housekeeping arrived with lightening-speed efficiency to restore order to the trauma room before the next onslaught of unthinkable horrors entered our lives. Kelly "whoever" was in the operating room for some final heroic surgical interventions, and those of us left behind began to move off to attend to other matters.

As the trauma room emptied, I asked John, one of the flight paramedics, what had happened, not sure I wanted to know but believing I needed to know to be able to assist Kelly's family when they arrived.

"We picked her up about a mile from the location of the accident. I'm not sure exactly what happened because we were never actually at the scene; however, what I was told was that she was hit by a train and dragged 150 feet down the tracks."

"Oh, my God," I thought to myself!

I hung around in the Emergency Department absentmindedly, trying to kill time as I waited for Kelly's family to arrive. Some of the staff went to chart; others went to register waiting patients, restock the trauma room, and care for others.

I distractedly laughed with staff as we saw one of our "frequent flyers," Walter, arrive on a stretcher, holding court much like Caesar the conquering hero arriving home from some great battle. I was grateful that the outbreak of activity had moved to the OR and yet I also was shocked by what I'd seen; not that I hadn't seen bodies in similar conditions before, but each time I see a human being torn apart and a life shattered, I am reminded of life's fragility and the tenuous threads by which it hangs. And yet, I, like all the rest of the staff, needed to keep going as there were other patients and families requiring care.

Anxiously, in my head I found I was repeating my mantra of "breathe" and in quick succession reviewing all of the stories of loss in which I'd been a part, almost like a life appraisal. As the time dragged by, it now carried a different sense of urgency.

After what seemed like an eternity, Kelly's parents arrived, anxious and strung as tight as strings on a violin. The registration clerk paged me and ushered the parents into the family conference room. Since I'd been anticipating their arrival, I knew when I received the page that it heralded their appearance. I took a couple of deep breaths and gratefully accepted the well wishes of staff as I headed off to meet Kelly's parents.

As I approached the family conference room I knew I was about to become a part of a parent's worst nightmare. I was keyed up because I anticipated the trajectory toward which they and I together would journey and ultimately they would travel alone to

One Train Track Too Many

deal with their daughter's death. As I entered the room, only the sound of their shallow breathing punctuated the silence as they waited for news that would forever change their lives.

I introduced myself, and they began to enfold me in their story of impending grief and loss; they told me about the morning's events and how all of this had come to pass. I shared with them all the empowering measures I knew to offer as they recited their all too familiar story; "Would you like some coffee, or can I get you some water? Is there anyone you'd like to call," I asked. "Would you like for us to have a prayer together?"

As we prayed, my pager went off. At the end of the prayer, I looked down and recognized the number as being the operating room, rarely announcing good news. All the welcoming behaviors I'd done upon their arrival suddenly seemed superfluous.

I excused myself long enough to call the operating room to tell the Trauma surgeon where I had the family. I went back into the conference room and told Kelly's parents that the surgeon attending their daughter was on his way down to talk with them.

A quick escape through self-hypnosis to my safe place for a moment of emotional respite was interrupted by a knock on the conference room door, which told me I needed to re-enter the nightmare into which I had ventured. Kelly's parents sat huddled together on the sofa, Dad reminding me of Ray, a man with whom I used to run as together we pounded the pavement for very different reasons, and in a similar fashion, Kelly's father was a man with whom I established an immediate connection and rapport.

Kelly's mother was less accessible and standoffish, with a seemingly flat and more detached affect. It was as though she was bothered to be here in "this place"; almost as if she were angry with Kelly for the way she had interrupted her day. I remained, perhaps lost or caught in the middle of an incomplete history; the parts of theirs and Kelly's life that might have been.

I could feel my own heightened disquiet rise and my own interior sense of horror swell as I introduced the doctor to Kelly's parents.

The news delivered: "I'm so sorry to tell you that your daughter did not survive."

The emergence of her parents' sadness and enveloping doom was only beginning to emerge and take shape. Dad, trying stoically to hold it together as he heard news of his baby girl while tears spilled from his eyes like dew that falls from the bell of a lily, spotting the front of his shirt. Huddled together on the sofa, yet seemingly worlds apart; each living in the throes of hopes, memories, prayers, and anticipated fears.

Kelly had been living at home on her parents' farm and had recently become engaged and was working as a secretary at a small business and was supposed to be there to open the office that morning as her boss was out of town. Dad told me that was what had taken them so long to get there. They had been trying to get ahold of Kelly's boss to make certain he didn't believe her to be untrustworthy since she wasn't there to open the office.

Kelly had slept through her alarm and was off to a later-than-normal start for work that morning. Railroad tracks ran at the edge of their farm parallel to the road leading to life apart from the family. That fateful morning Kelly ran out of the door and jumped into her car, radio playing music at a volume intended to wake the dead. Her coffee rested in the center console, and Kelly's determination to make it to work on time despite the lateness of her departure hung like a tattered banner as it now pointlessly flapped in the breeze.

... The directions to a new life of marriage, now a road leading to a life for those left behind marked by soul-shattering grief.

Time, the illusive, the inescapable, binding us to a world of predictable realities: trains travel faster than cars ...

A quick leap of the car across the tracks and home free to make it to work on time . . . A blaring whistle punctuated the morning silence as metal collided with metal . . . Wheels screeching on tracks pushed a car and person down the tracks into a different kind of reality altogether . . . The assurance and impetuosity of youth; plans for a future that will never come to be, thoughts of

One Train Track Too Many

a wedding which will never take place. Gone with the recklessness of a short life lived on the edge . . .

Chapter 19

The Smell of Flesh

The smell of burning flesh wafted through the air with its sort of sickly sweet acrid odor as the cauterizing instrument sealed off the worst of the "bleeders" and a few sutures were taken to make sure the artery wouldn't spring forth like a geyser once pressure was removed. A quick trip to the operating room later would create enough of a flap that perhaps a prosthetic devise could be fitted.

It was early on what promised to be a warm spring day in Richmond. If you were watching the traffic snake its way down River Road you likely would have seen many arms protruding from open vehicle windows as people enjoyed the first breath of a burgeoning spring.

Shirley left home that morning headed to work . . . Shirley was probably someone who had never shopped in a petite section except as a young child—maybe! She always loved the early morning drive as she could fully inhale the intoxicating first hits of nicotine and feel the caffeine rush as she enjoyed her morning cigs and coffee.

When the weather was Spring-like, it was hard not to enjoy the beauty of the flowers. Her coffee was wedged against her left

The Smell of Flesh

leg, and the radio was blaring music for her to feel alive; good dance music.

Shirley loved nothing better than to drive with her left arm hanging out of the window when the weather was nice holding her cigarette pursed between her lips. She relished the feeling of the wind rushing through her fingers as she occasionally held her cigarette in her left hand and took a couple of quick gulps of her hot coffee (a little cream and three sugars) with her right hand while gripping the steering wheel with her knees.

While reveling in this morning ritual, Shirley ventured too close to the side of the road, and her right front tire went off the edge of the pavement. No problem! Who among us hasn't become distracted and had a wheel go over the line, followed by the accompanying correction to get back on track?

The next thing Shirley knew her car was airborne, taking an unwelcomed flight as she flipped over and over again down an embankment, finally coming to rest on the driver's side. A phantom pain shot through her left arm–an arm which was no more! Her arm severed, clean as a whistle right at the joint and spurting blood.

Fortunately the road upon which she had been traveling was fairly well traveled at that time of day, and the driver of a tractor-trailer who had seen her vehicle leave the blacktop stopped; the Good Samaritan staunched the flow of blood using the skirt of Shirley's new summer print dress, and another passing vehicle called 911.

Shirley's extrication took almost two hours because of the location and condition of the vehicle. The paramedics also struggled to locate her missing arm, which had become wedged in some underbrush beneath her car.

Meanwhile, I was holding down a chair in a somewhat boring faculty meeting when my trauma pager sounded forth. On occasion I would get one of the clinical pastoral education residents to cover calls for the Emergency Department when I had meetings; however, this particular morning they had an educational event to attend, so I had agreed to carry the trauma pager. Because we have a ten-minute required response time, I rose abruptly, told my colleagues I needed to go, and headed down the stairs and out the back door of the building in which the program was housed. I had to make tracks to make it in the specified time.

I arrived at the door to the Emergency Department about the same time the Henrico Rescue crew was rolling in, moving pretty briskly. Accompanying them was a large ice chest carried by two EMTs, and I remembered thinking that was a bit odd at the time. Why would they be bringing an ice chest along with a patient on a gurney? The sheets covering what I assumed to be a body were fairly well saturated with blood. One of my friends was the paramedic on the team, and I recognized Chris from having done his wedding the previous year. As we rolled into trauma bed 1, the location for the most critical of patients, Chris began spouting off info regarding the patient's condition and what had transpired so far.

As the nurses hung blood to replace the depleted volume the trauma docs made certain that Shirley's vital signs were stable and all the "bleeders" were tied off. Sue, one of the trauma nurses, hollered at me and asked if I would grab a couple of blankets out of the warmer. This was when I had my first introduction to Shirley, who lay stark naked, having had her clothes cut off, and who was strapped to a backboard. I gently spread the warm blankets over her exposed flesh, returning a sense of purposeful dignity to a clearly chaotic blood bath. I took Shirley's remaining hand in mine as in revulsion I caught sight of the place where her left arm once had been. I almost wretched and had to slow chest breathe as the image of exposed yellowish fatty tissue etched itself in my memory.

I averted my eyes from the location of her missing arm and introduced myself to Shirley and offered her two fingers to hold. I assured her that I would remain present with her. She began asking me questions about how she'd gotten here and what had happened. I told her what I knew so far, which was very little, and I explained to her what had been done to help her to this point. Shirley looked at me with somewhat glassy eyes as though I were from some

The Smell of Flesh

distant planet but gave a feeble smile of gratitude as I began to reassure her that she was doing okay! I was informed by my friend Chris that someone at the scene had contacted Shirley's family and told them where she had been taken; a brother, he believed, who lived out of state and wouldn't be there for several hours, but was on his way. Shirley was now a foreigner in a strange place.

When there were clinical pastoral education students in the trauma room with me, I frequently asked them to consider, and try and imagine, what it would be like to travel to a foreign land where they did not speak the language. I would tell them that for most patients entering the hospital, it was like traveling to an undisclosed location. I told them that our job as chaplains was to purvey not only God's grace, love, and the holiness of life, but also to become interpreters for those who might be under-resourced in understanding the jargon of health care.

As such, I became Shirley's interpreter, keeping her apprised of who various people were, along with their roles and what they were attempting to do to and for her. The orthopedic attending physician arrived, looked at Shirley's open wound, and declared that it looked good and that they would be taking her to the operating room later that day to clean out the wound additionally. The attending physician opened the ice chest to peer at its contents, and there was Shirley's arm on ice. I'd previously seen fingers brought to the ED wrapped in tissues, but somehow those occasions paled and were different from viewing an entire arm on ice!

The orthopedist, after inspecting the arm, told Shirley that they would not be able to reattach it. That was that! Simple! No fuss, no muss! The arm simply was . . . gone. A moment's poor judgment, a faulty decision, and in the twinkling of an eye a life changed. Shirley's words to me: "I think I'm going to be giving up smoking now."

While there are those who claim that denial is not a river in Egypt, I'm not sure if what I saw that day was denial, shock, or some form of disassociation. But whatever it was, it seemed to be working for Shirley at that moment as she sought to create a new "normal" for her life. I asked if she would like for us to have a prayer. She said, "yes," and together we prayed for healing and courage. I'm not sure who needed the prayer more, her or perhaps me.

Since that day, I don't believe I've driven with an arm outside of my car window, and somehow I doubt that I ever will!

Chapter 20

Jailed

One of the challenges of working as a hospital chaplain in a community hospital was that I rarely made sufficient income and often had to pick up extra work. For a part of the time that I lived in Charleston, West Virginia, I worked as a chaplain at St. Francis Hospital, a small Catholic community facility. While in that role, I also served as temporary pastor for a small Presbyterian church outside of town about fifteen miles and I also was moonlighting, working for CORE (the Center for Organ Recovery and Education), whose home office was located in Pittsburgh, Pennsylvania.

I became a designated requestor for organ, tissue, and eye donation back in the early 1990s and had worked formerly for Lifenet in Virginia as well as the Arkansas Organ Recovery Agency. Working for CORE was simply having the opportunity to do once again that for which previously I had been trained and from which I drew a great deal of satisfaction.

As a chaplain at St. Francis I was required to take call for the hospital every other weekend, which meant responding to any deaths or other requests for a chaplain. Ordinarily I rarely received any calls but always remained prepared, just in case. This particular weekend proved to be anything but ordinary!

Through the Eyes of the Heart

About 11 on Saturday morning I received a call from the ICU at St. Francis telling me that one of the patients with whom I'd been working during the previous week was actively dying. His family members, with whom I'd developed a rapport, were at his bedside and asked if I would come and be present with them as their father died. It took me about half an hour to shower, get dressed, and drive to the hospital which, thank goodness, was only a hop, skip, and a jump away from my home.

Upon my arrival at the hospital I went straight to the ICU. It was early spring, cool but not cold, with the smell of apple blossoms wafting on the gentle breezes. I went in and checked with the nurse who was caring for Mr. X just to garner a sense of what was going on for him and his family. His family was gathered around his bedside, sitting quietly and peacefully observing the rise and fall of his chest.

I went into the patient's room and offered hugs around to Mr. X's family and checked to see how they were. We shared a prayer and sat and talked as they shared stories about Mr. X as a young man. Shortly after my arrival, my cell phone rang, and I stepped out into the hallway to take the call. It was Kurt S., my supervisor from CORE, asking me to please head over to Women and Children's Hospital, located about a block away from St. Francis. He asked me to go over and do an assessment on a 4-year-old male to determine if the child was a suitable candidate as a potential organ donor.

Assessing that Mr. X still had some time before his death, I excused myself, asking the nurse to call me when and if Mr. X looked as if he was getting closer to dying. I jumped in my car and headed over to Women and Children's hospital. I'd never been in that particular facility before as most of the donor families with whom I'd worked were adults and were almost always located at Charleston Area Medical Center.

Fortunately when I arrived at the Pediatric Intensive Care Unit, one of the nurses with whom I'd previously worked, was on duty taking care of Nate. Lucky for me because she helped steer me through their system to obtain the information that I needed. The

Jailed

Pediatric Intensive Care physician happened to be present on the unit as well, and it was she who had initiated the call to CORE to evaluate Nate as a potential candidate for donation.

After a brief discussion with her and the nurse and having called in some key lab values to Kurt, I was given the "go ahead" to proceed. The physician indicated that she believed Nate already was "brain dead." I told her that for me to continue, she needed to conduct "brain death testing" and the family needed to have been informed about what the test results revealed.

She indicated that they hadn't yet conducted "brain death testing" and wondered exactly what needed to be done. I explained the different procedures approved for brain death testing, and she initiated the process, leaving me to decipher "the tangled web" of family, trying to determine exactly who was the next of kin.

Why that proved to be such a challenge was that in this particular situation Nate's mother was in prison serving a five-year sentence for selling drugs, and Nate's biological father, while having lived with the mother, was not legally married to her. And while grandparents were present, they held no legal standing since the birth mother was living.

An additional complicating factor in this unfolding drama was the fact that it was Nate's father, with whom he'd been living, who was believed to have been the perpetrator of the injuries to Nate. If in fact that was the case, he would be charged with murder making this case a homicide to boot . . .

As I waited for confirmatory testing of brain death, Amy, the nurse from St. Francis, called to tell me that Mr. X was actively dying. So once again I jumped in my car and headed back to St. Francis, arriving just in time to be with his family as he took his last breaths and died peacefully, surrounded by a loving family.

I prayed with the family of Mr. X and assisted them with funeral arrangements, all the while hoping that perhaps by the time I got back to Women's and Children's the physician would have completed the initial steps toward declaring Nate brain dead. I escorted Mr. X's family from the hospital jumped in my car, and proceeded back to Women's and Children's, hoping I could finish up the consent process quickly so I could return home at a reasonable hour and get a good night's rest so that I would be prepared to conduct worship on Sunday morning.

When I arrived back at Women's and Children's Hospital, the nurse told me that the first set of testing for brain death indeed had confirmed their suspicions that Nate was dead. The staff had gone ahead and contacted the sheriff's office, and deputies were on their way to arrest Nate's father.

In my absence, they also had made arrangements for Nate's mother to be brought to the hospital from prison, which was located several hours from Charleston, to say her goodbyes. She was now the parent from whom I would need to obtain consent for donation. Unlikely, but you just never know; I'd been surprised before.

Nate, a beautiful, young vivacious 4-year-old, the product of two extremely challenged adults, now fodder . . . (It's tough for me to maintain a sense of objectivity and detachment when I come face to face with the kind of life this young child must have lived. Perhaps he was fortunate to have died so young! My value judgments were going crazy making assumptions as though I were God.)

I contacted the medical examiner for Kanawha County, and the physician and I together talked them through what next steps we would like to take. The medical examiner advised that under no circumstances should the mother be allowed to touch Nate's body when she arrived in the hopes of protecting any forensic evidence needed to support the murder charges to be brought against Nate's father. It was the staff's considered opinion based on Nate's pattern of bruising that he had died from being shaken vigorously.

However, I was given permission to take his mother and grandparents in to view Nate's body and to say their goodbyes. Even though Mom was still several hours out, I had to continue to monitor Nate's body as it remained on mechanical supports. Additionally, I had a set of prescribed orders to place in the chart designed to maintain the viability of Nate's organs for potential transplant . . .

Jailed

Around 6 p.m. Nate's mother finally arrived, surrounded by two guards and chained to a fare-thee-well. Upon seeing Mom it was easy to see where Nate got his good looks as she was an exceptionally pretty woman with gorgeous strawberry blonde hair. I have to say she was not what I expected. I had made her out to be a real villain in my mind. Instead, she looked much more like a young, innocent woman who got caught up in some crazy behaviors and life circumstances.

I sat and visited with Carla, Nate's mom, for quite a while. She sobbed about her lack of judgment for having left Nate in his father's care, and she disparaged and belittled herself for ever having become involved with such a low life. She told me that she believed Nate had been one of the few good outcomes that had ever been a part of her life. She expressed suicidal thoughts and indicated that she had nothing else for which to live; a concern, but not mine at the moment.

Nate's grandparents, Carla's parents, were also present. Her mother, Nate's grandmother, was beside herself with grief and was as kind as she could be to Carla, whose son was now dead. As I began to formulate my approach to Carla about organ donation, I decided to approach her from the idea of not letting Nate's life have been in vain.

Initially when I asked for her consent for Nate to be an organ donor, she told me, "hell no!" She didn't want her baby cut on; he had suffered enough. When I explained to her that the medical examiner had the right to do an autopsy and was planning on doing one anyway because of the pending murder charges, I told her that when they did the autopsy that Nate's organs then would simply be wasted. She changed her mind and said that she would rather some other parent not have to go through what she was going through.

I've learned over time to give people the time they need to grieve before trying to rush them into decisions. And I've found that presented with all of the information, people frequently will make decisions to help others. By the time Carla finally made the decision for Nate to donate, it was approaching midnight and the deputies who had brought Carla from the prison were anxious to get her back. I went with Carla to say her goodbyes from the doorway to her son. My heart ached for them both. Not only had Nate's life been wasted, but so had those of his father and mother alike.

It didn't matter what the courts found; none of them would ever recover from the horror of this trauma!

Epilogue

As I reflect upon my life, I have been richly blessed with the gifts of both love and loss. Each of these stories has touched and moved me time and time again. As I wrote them, I relived them and once again experienced the sense of awe, wonder, sadness, and the heart wrenching awareness of the fragility of life and the depth to which it is replete with ever-changing circumstances.

None of our lives is static; but each moves in different ways with the ebb and flow of life's circumstances as we encounter them. Through the years I've met precious few people whose lives have followed a narrowly focused trajectory, and I've met even fewer people who remain untouched by their experiences of love and loss if they remain open to the challenges which come their way.

One of the ways in which I've been affected by my journey is that I take very little for granted in life, recognizing that this moment is the only one I have. I live life with a focus on gratitude and with eyes turned toward the future with only an occasional glance back at the past.

When I do take that backward glance, I see the distant reflection of a person barely recognizable as me today. I've had the experience of being challenged, at times forced into growth and new awareness with which I've learned to live. As I've wrestled with emotional turmoil prompted by various challenges and persons who have been part of my life, frequently, I've felt like a pretzel-man, contorted, emotionally disassembled, and cast forth on the sands of time to begin anew; a new way of thinking, occasionally jaded, along with a new, improved, and broadened perspective. While I wouldn't wish many of the experiences of my professional life on anyone, at this point in time, I'm grateful for the lessons I've learned, the people I've loved, the people who have loved me, those with whom I've had the privilege of journeying, and those who have enriched my life, in a variety of unexpected ways.

www.ingramcontent.com/pod-product-compliance
Lightning Source LLC
Chambersburg PA
CBHW070509090426
42735CB00012B/2713